C000240720

Judith Dimond is a lay member of
Church in Canterbury, and a Companion of the
St Francis. Retired now from work in both the public and
voluntary sectors, she divides her time between writing poetry
(some of which has been published in anthologies and jour-
nals) and her family life. This centres around her daughters,
two lively grandchildren, and a large extended family. She lives
with her husband in what was once a pub, and together they
enjoy exploring the coasts of Kent and Northern France. She is
also the author of *Gazing on the Gospels, Year B* (SPCK, 2008)
and *Gazing on the Gospels, Year A* (forthcoming, SPCK, 2010).

GAZING ON THE GOSPELS YEAR C

Meditations on the Lectionary readings

Judith Dimond

First published in Great Britain in 2009

Society for Promoting Christian Knowledge
36 Causton Street
London SW1P 4ST

British Library Cataloguing-in-Publication Data
A catalogue record for this book is available from the British Library

ISBN 978–0–281–06121–1

1 3 5 7 9 10 8 6 4 2

Typeset by Graphicraft Ltd, Hong Kong
Printed in Great Britain by Ashford Colour Press

Produced on paper from sustainable forests

To Keith, in celebration of our fortieth anniversary

'A husband of noble character . . .
worth far more than rubies.'
(Proverbs 31.10, adapted)

Contents

———•◆•———

Acknowledgements

My continued gratitude must be expressed to Revd Canon Paul Cox for all his wisdom and guidance: Proverbs 1.2–5.

The quotation on p. 38 is by Rainer Maria Rilke, translated by J. B. Leishman, from POSSIBILITY OF BEING, copyright © 1977 by New Directions Publishing Corp. Reprinted by permission of New Directions Publishing Corp.

The quotation on p. 39 is taken from *The Cloud of Unknowing and Other Works*, trans. by Clifton Wolters (Harmondsworth: Penguin, 1961), Chapter 6, p. 68.

Introduction

This is the second in the series of Gospel reflections following the Anglican Church's lectionary, and it follows the same simple pattern as before, which even busy people can find time for as they approach Sunday. It will take no more time to read than would a quick scan of the headlines, but it will take much longer for the words of the Gospel to work within us to bring about self-examination and understanding. And this is why a pattern of reflection is so helpful. The advice of Clare of Assisi in her second letter to Agnes of Prague is:

Gaze on him
Consider him
Contemplate him
As you desire to imitate him

The use of the mirror as a means to contemplation was central to Clare's prayer life. She challenged herself, her sisters, and ourselves, to gaze deeper and deeper and see reflected in the mirror the poverty, humility and charity of Jesus. Contemplation of our Lord should be our 'refreshment', for we must contemplate his glory as well as our sins. Our blemished face must gaze into the unblemished face of Christ until we finally take on his image. Using this pattern helps us exercise our senses and our intellect, and helps us look outward to the world as well as inward to our souls. It enables the social gospel to be examined as well as the spiritual path to be followed.

During Year C, we concentrate our gospel gaze on Jesus as described by Luke. What I have come to appreciate by going through these readings is the great power of Luke's storytelling, which includes some of our best loved parables found only here, including the Good Samaritan and the Prodigal Son. How unthinkable it would be to teach and preach the gospel of Jesus today without either of these great stories.

Another impact of working through Luke has been to make me aware of the great theme of reversal within the Gospel, and the challenge to our security and complacency. This reversal is evident in the repeated overturning of the accepted world order, of the first being last, and the times when the obvious candidates for this world's reward are rejected in God's Kingdom in favour of the little 'insignificant' person. The good news is that this reversal 'is not for destruction of the wicked but for the saving of the lost',[1] another reason why the tale of the Prodigal Son joins the story of the lost sheep and lost coin in Luke.

For those new to the structure of this book, I set out below a brief outline of how to use St Clare's wise words:

Gaze on him

With all your senses: what do you see, hear, smell, feel and taste? So many of Luke's stories are full of vivid detail. Imagine you are part of the story. Listen to the tone of voice of Jesus and his opponents, or Jesus and his petitioners. What does that tell you? Other passages can by opened up by gazing not on the story itself, but on a related or surprising image taken from our own age and experience.

Consider him

Examine and expand the story to make connections within your life and the world around you. This is when it can be so helpful to notice the place of each story in the sequence as the Gospel was written, which is not always the order our lectionary uses. So at times I refer to the passage which precedes or follows in the Gospel which we may not have read, but it sheds great light on the value of the portion. Alternatively, it can be helpful to remember its place in the lectionary cycle, and as a layperson I know it is not easy at all to remember what was read the week before, and carry the connection forward.

Contemplate him

In your heart, deepen your personal relationship with Jesus as you meditate on the passage, and deepen its meaning to you today. When you look into St Clare's mirror, do you see yourself as you would be content for Jesus to see you, or do you only notice the shadows that set you apart? How can you ensure that the differences dwindle, and the resemblance grows?

As you desire to imitate him

We are being pressed by Luke to 'change (our) social behaviour in imitation of God'[2] and so, after our gazing, considering and contemplation, we must focus in prayer on our desire to imitate our Lord. This imitation is a way of being which includes in it the determination to act in the world and so contribute to the great reversal that Jesus came to earth to bring about – reversal of the consequences of sin, reversal of the distorted and corrupt values of this world to a just and sharing society, and reversal to a humanity which shines with delight in God's glory.

Notes

1 Luke Timothy Johnson, *Sacra Pagina: The Gospel of Luke* (Collegeville, MN: The Liturgical Press, 1990), Introduction.
2 See note 1.

ADVENT

The First Sunday of Advent

Luke 21.25–36

Gaze on all the climate change nightmares we read about – mountains sliding into rivers, icebergs breaking off from the Antarctic mass; rising sea levels and waves breaching sea defences, and winds that upend ancient oaks. Is this the final cataclysm that Jesus describes, when God's power will overwhelm our trite existence? Gaze on these scenes, as frightening as Dante's depiction of hell, or as alarming as Michelangelo's judgement paintings. Are we about to bring these to life? We may have forgotten the fear of hell which plagued the people of the Middle Ages, but we still know the anguish of nations suffering hells of our own making.

Consider how the season of Advent is one where gloom predominates, just as it does in our weather, when the nights are long and the days are dreary. Jesus seems to emphasize this mood in his warning to us, telling us how he expects us to lead our lives, in anticipation of this cataclysm. In verse 34 he lists three behaviours to avoid. First, we must not be weighed down by dissipation. Most of us think of wild orgies when we hear this word, and could say, 'Well, I'm OK there, I don't go in for that sort of thing.' But to dissipate is also to squander, scatter or fritter away – time, money, energy or resources – and we are all guilty of that, both in our personal and our economic life. Is it not exactly such behaviour which has brought about global warming? Next, Jesus singles out our drunkenness, and again we might say, 'Phew, I'm OK, I don't drink to excess; I've never been charged with drink-driving.' So, we think we're all right, alert enough to recognize the signs of the new age. Well, no actually, because Jesus links with these two moral failings another one – anxiety.

Consider why this is mentioned in the same breath as dissipation and drunkenness. To be anxious means we believe we should keep what we have, and that yesterday owes us tomorrow – a false notion that the poor have never entertained. Deep down, we know we are not in control, and are desperate to find somewhere solid to place our trust. Give up false expectations, Jesus tells us, and rely on him. Then we will be open enough to greet the new creation.

Consider how this message is for nations as well as individuals.

Contemplate all that you have accumulated in your life, and take a moment to distinguish between what is of lasting worth, and what plays no part in living a life in readiness for the Kingdom. Contemplate all that you have dissipated. Contemplate the one constant in our world: the words of Christ (v. 33). Absolute truth cannot be altered by storm or catastrophe, and is not afraid of judgement.

As you prepare through Advent, spend time reducing your anxiety, and increasing your reliance on God – watch, and pray.

As you desire to imitate him

Unchanging God, help me lead a simple, holy life
Without dissipation of my energy
Or excess of trivial pleasure
Or anxiety about my possessions.
Open my heart to interpret
The signs of summer in the depths of winter,
So I will be able to stand before the Son of Man.
Amen.

The Second Sunday of Advent

Luke 3.1–6

Gaze on a lone hiker, setting out on a long distance walk in the Lake District, or Scottish highlands, perhaps. Imagine it's you, dressed in the latest Gore-Tex® to keep out the wind and rain, waterproof trousers already on, sturdy climbing boots laced on your feet, a heavy haversack on your back and a pole tightly gripped in your hand. You'll need a compass and a map, but still the way forward isn't sure, for there have been landslips that bar the route and you're forced to double back, taking much longer than planned. Each hill promises the summit, but once you get there and catch your breath, you find another hill beyond. Now the fog is rolling down, hiding the path. Thirsty, dirty and tired, you've got miles to cover before reaching the shelter where you planned to pitch your tent. Wouldn't you join in Isaiah's song, and long for the hills to be made low, and the rough ways smooth?

Consider the list of names at the beginning of this reading. It is as if Luke is reciting a roll call of all the greats of first-century Palestine. He seems determined to convince the reader that all this really happened. He is grounding this story in historical fact. These men were real, so why doubt that John and Jesus were real too?

Consider also the tremendous contrast displayed between all these powerful men who thought they were in charge of the world, and John. For look who is coming over the horizon – far from palace, fort or parliament, not even attached to church or temple. God chooses to act for him a simple man named John, who knows that the silence of the wilderness is the place to hear the Word of God. However sincere leaders are, whatever their policies or strategies, however many white or green papers and statutes politicians enact, despite all this well-meaning activity, they never seem able to transform society. To do that, we must start silently, within ourselves.

Contemplate in silence the wildest place you have ever been. Sit in that place – is it cold, or hot, touching the sky or a deep, deep cave? How do you feel there? Silence and simplicity can often feel threatening, as deep truths emerge unbidden. What does God want to tell you – about yourself, the people you live with, the wider world you move in? What crooked corners of your heart does God want to make straight?

As you desire to imitate him

God of Judgement, may I be ready
To follow John into the wilderness,
For all my rough ways to be made smooth,
So that I can serve in your world
And be part of the solution,
Not the problem.
Amen.

The Third Sunday of Advent

Luke 3.7–18

Gaze on all these people arriving at last by the river where John is busy baptizing the penitents. They run on eagerly, but when they get within earshot, they rock back on their heels, as he explodes 'You brood of vipers!' Is it for this that they came, to be insulted instead of welcomed? Some drift off quite quickly, back home, unwilling to be treated this way. Others stay a little longer, but give up at the severity of John's pronouncements. Listen to the force behind his words. Listen to their tone of accusation. See the images he conjures up of wrath, the axe, and the unquenchable fire. We are being judged here, and whether we stay or go, the judgement will stand.

Consider God's judgement on our complacency. It is not enough to hope we can fade into the background and not be noticed. We must go forward and let John plunge us into the Jordan. We must live lives that give evidence of a real repentance. John won't let us rely on any claims to shelter in the shadow of Abraham. In other words, it won't be enough to say 'But I'm a Jew' or 'I'm a Christian, I go to church, so I'm safe, aren't I?' Each one of us must make a personal commitment to obey God's ordinance. And in order to restore my relationship with God, I must restore my relationship with my sisters and brothers. Just as we're stocking the larder for Christmas and shopping for presents, we hear again the lesson Jesus taught in Luke 21.25–36 (see p. 2), that greed, lust and a life weighed down by excessive accumulation are anathema.

All very depressing, isn't it? Yet at the end of this frightening diatribe, how is it that John describes the message he brings? As good news! Good news is more than a little obscured in this passage, but we find it in the prediction that when 'the one to come' is here, he will bring a baptism which will save.

Contemplate facing God – head bare and hands empty. We can bring nothing on Judgement Day to bribe him with. All the good deeds we have done will not be enough. Nor will we be able to beg for a second chance. We cannot flee from the 'coming wrath'. We can only repent and pray for baptism by the Holy Spirit.

Contemplate the urgency of John's message. What must you set about changing in your life *today*?

As you desire to imitate him

God of Abraham, let me take seriously your warning
That judgement is part of your salvation plan.
Help me search my heart for the thoughts which you deplore
And for the actions that turn me away from you.
May I hear John's warnings and repent,
May I know Jesus' good news and be saved.
Amen.

The Fourth Sunday of Advent

---◆---

Luke 1.39–45 [46–55]

Gaze on a woman in pregnancy. At the beginning, when the baby first moves, it is a secret known only to the mother, then shared with her partner, family and close friends, and in time, the domed belly will force all around to know that a new life is about to appear in the world. The way the woman holds her hands, palms spread, over the stretched skin, as if protecting the baby within, makes it obvious. Her hands are always in communication with the baby, feeling its twists and turns, the times it leaps in the womb. Gaze on Elizabeth, older in years, more advanced in her pregnancy, greeting her young cousin, Mary. Had rumours of Mary's predicament already reached her, or was her arrival the first time she learnt of this second baby? Here are two women, expecting the miracle of childbirth for the first time in their lives, full of trepidation. But all those worries dissolve when the baby moves and new life is felt.

Consider how intimate these details are, so intimate that only Mary and Elizabeth could have told Luke this story. For these precious moments of childbearing are never forgotten by women, however many years pass, and whatever happens in between. The time of pregnancy is unique.

Consider what Luke is trying to express here: that the miracle of the incarnation was so amazing that even the baby in Elizabeth's womb recognized the specialness of Mary's baby before he was born. The incarnation itself is at first a secret known to only a husband and a cousin. But over the Christmas

8

and Epiphany seasons we are about to enter, that secret will little by little be broadcast to every nation.

Consider the hope given us all in verse 45: 'Blessed is she who has believed that what the Lord has said to her will be accomplished.' Mary, finally realizing the enormity of what God is doing through her, makes the most amazing leap and links her personal history with the rise and fall of rulers, the experiences of the rich and poor. If we have the faith and trust that Mary had, we too can believe that what the Lord has promised will be accomplished in our lives. So much of today's discontent stems from the existential fear that we count for nothing. So Mary's story can be ours, and tells each one of us that, however unlikely we consider it, we count in God's plan.

Contemplate how Mary realizes that in some mysterious way, past, present and future will all be affected by this birth. Contemplate how in the birth of Jesus, hope will become reality; the hope that comes with each birth and every new life, the surge of optimism that 'all will be well' (Dame Julian of Norwich), is not any more forgotten, but brought to fulfilment.

As you desire to imitate him

Great and Mighty God, help me make Mary's song of hope
    my own.
May I be on the side of the humble and the hungry
And work to overturn the power of the proud and the rich.
May your will for me and for the world be accomplished,
Through the grace of your son, Jesus Christ.
Amen.

CHRISTMAS

Christmas Day

John 1.1–14

Gaze on the darkness of the midnight sky over a rough sea. Gaze on a lighthouse, painted bright white, seeming to grow out of the rocky island it is built upon. This is not a place of safety. Waves lash the rocks, the wind roars and spray covers you with salt. Picture the shipwrecks that occurred here before the lighthouse was built, the sailors and passengers who lost their lives and never reached their destination. Now gaze on the pulse of light that emanates from its powerful lamps. The wide beam trembles on the unquiet waves. Here is a light to rescue the traveller, a light that shines in the darkness, a light with a life-saving task.

Consider how tough the last four weeks' readings have been. We've been immersed in terrible visions and harangued and placed in the dock and found guilty. John's Gospel starts with accepting that we inhabit a place of darkness and confusion. But today is a day of hope. Consider the number of times the word light appears in this piece – seven; darkness appears only twice. We need not be conquered by our present age. In these opening verses, John is encapsulating everything he believed Jesus' life was about, and he sets down in miniature all that will follow in his Gospel. No wonder this passage is arguably the best known and best loved in the whole New Testament. And what is the last word of all in this passage? It is *truth*. A truth not afraid of light and a truth that will save the world. A truth contained in flesh and in the word.

Contemplate quietly for a few moments. Go and find a candle, and light it now. If you can, pull the curtains and sit in the dark. Contemplate the sturdy flame, how it twists and turns but always seeks to remain upright, to reach for heaven. It bends to the draughts, and is never still, but always seeks its centre. It stretches out to its fullest height. It seems to breathe, it is pulsing with an inner life. This is the flame of truth.

As you desire to imitate him

Light of the world, help me recognize
The light of your messengers – to show the way,
The light of your word – to teach me wisdom,
The light that others bring – the gift of love,
The light when sincere prayer is heard – the light of grace.
So may we see your glory in the light of Jesus.
Amen.

The First Sunday of Christmas

Luke 2.41–52

Gaze on the chaos of a pilgrimage – the coaches lined up one by one in the car park, people trying to remember which their coach was, and do they recognize the driver? Imagine Mary and Joseph, missing Jesus, but confident he's with another member of the extended family, perhaps with his cousins or uncles. They know he's a sensible boy, and quite grown up now, so no need to worry, just yet.

Gaze on the other young twelve-year-olds from Nazareth, who had gone reluctantly to Jerusalem. They are apprehensive, for soon they will be expected to participate as an adult in the religious community. They are anxious that it means they must soon calm down, leave their games behind and begin to grow up.

Gaze on this young boy, sitting in the Temple, polite but not shy, as willing to talk as he is to listen. He is so engrossed, he doesn't know the time, and completely forgets his parents are waiting for him. Gaze on the elders, their eyebrows raised, amazed at this boy who engages the teachers in conversation as an equal.

Consider the astonishment of Mary and Joseph: their growing realization that their son is different. Mary and Joseph remember the strange predictions that surrounded his birth, and it begins to dawn on them that the past twelve years have been an oasis of calm, a period of waiting and preparation. But now events are out of their hands.

14

Yet consider how little time Jesus seems to spend in his Father's house in the Gospels, for more often we meet him on the road, in the fields, or eating in someone's home. But remember, the Gospels only tell us about three years of his life. What, we wonder, did he do in the years between his pilgrimage to the Temple and his baptism in the Jordan? We suppose he worked for his father as a carpenter. But maybe he spent all his spare time in the synagogue and followed the teachers wherever they were as often as his father could spare him, to discuss and deliberate and delve into the Torah. For him to have had such a command of his Scriptures and for them to have become the resource and anchor that they were once his ministry began, he must have been immersed in them.

Consider who you share your ideas with. Is it enough to listen to the sermon most Sundays, or should you be finding other ways to discuss the faith, and grow in wisdom?

Contemplate being in the house of God – think of the church you find most holy, where you find it most easy to pray. Remember the feel of the wooden pew under your hands, the smell of the polish; the flower arrangement by that stained-glass window, the light falling through, showing up minute specks of dust floating in the air; the sparkle of the brass; the dazzling white behind the altar, the simple cross placed at its centre, symbol of the Son's presence.

Rest a while in this place and feel yourself draw near to God.

As you desire to imitate him

Dear Father, strengthen my resolve
To spend time with you;
To sit quietly each day
And gaze on your presence
To consider your word
And contemplate your will for me.
Amen.

The Second Sunday of Christmas

John 1.[1–9]10–18

Gaze on all of God's glorious creation, at once so mysterious and yet so familiar. It is hard to find an image today that captures the carefulness of God's work, for we are in a world where everything is mass produced, and we are removed from the manufacturing process. Even if we work in a factory, we only see a part of the final creation. Very, very few of us work as once the craftsmen did who built our magnificent cathedrals, when stonemasons carefully carved the pillars and poured all their creative energies into their work. It is in our hobbies today that we try to share in the experience of creation. We want to design and model something outside of ourselves – tend a garden, ice a cake, sing in a choir, or paint a picture. When we are absorbed in doing something we really love, we get as close as we ever can to the wonder of the Creator, and the deliberate passion of creation.

Consider the date when you are reading this – in or around New Year's Day, a time of new beginnings. How do you feel on New Year's Eve – do you rejoice at the passing of the old, or embrace the year ahead, a year of fresh chances and opportunities to join in the act of creation? We need to keep a sense of excitement that something new can happen, just as John had predicted. For the incarnation was a new creation and the inauguration of a new world, one dominated by the grace and truth of Jesus. Grace is love undeserved, and truth is the gift of wisdom which learning alone cannot bring. These are the blessings we read of in verse 16, the Christmas gifts bestowed through the Word becoming flesh. So when we compose our new year resolutions, we must make sure they are ambitions directed to God's glory and in tune with God's word to us in Jesus.

Contemplate the final verse here: 'No one has ever seen God, but God the One and Only, who is at the Father's side, has made him known.' Breathe in the assurance this gives in times when you struggle with faith and feel far from God. If we follow the infant Jesus as he grows and walks among us, we will know the presence of God.

As you desire to imitate him

One and Only God, if I receive you into my heart
And believe in your name
I will become your child.
From the fullness of your grace
May I be blessed this new year
And all the year ahead.
Amen.

EPIPHANY

The First Sunday of Epiphany

———•◆•———

Luke 3.15–17, 21–22

Gaze at the audience in a theatre, all waiting expectantly for their favourite pop singer to stride on stage, the one and only who's flown over from America for the first time in ten years; this is a once in a lifetime opportunity to see her in the flesh. Will she live up to expectations? There is an air of excitement and hubbub of conversation as people settle into their seats. The lights dim and the drums roll. Gradually a hush spreads through the auditorium; the curtain rises and the stage is flooded with light.

Consider how excited some people get when celebrities are in town and how our media is absorbed by their lives. Is it to try to experience vicariously some of their glamour, that readers and viewers concentrate so hard on every detail of their lives? Is it an indictment of the emptiness of their own lives that they long to be associated with the 'A list'? And yet the cult of celebrity is so precarious. One foot wrong and they are banished from the news and even if they pander to the whim of their fans, they can never be sure they will not be supplanted by a younger, more beautiful or more shocking individual. Our society has lost the ability to be faithful, and confused the reality of a hero with the shallowness of fame.

The bands of preachers and healers travelling Judea at the time of Christ were the celebrities of their day. In an age where there was no TV, and no organized entertainment, the appearance of such leaders must have been a red-letter day indeed.

When you add to this mix their hope that one of these charismatic rabbis might actually be the Messiah, then you can understand how intoxicating the fervour must have been.

It is an unusual celebrity who will willingly relinquish centre stage. But this is what John does; he steps off to the wings and leaves Jesus in the limelight. And there he has remained for 2,000 years.

Contemplate the difference between a celebrity, a hero and a saviour. Someone can be a celebrity for all the wrong reasons. He or she is certainly shown in glory, but there is no 'epiphany', no revelation of anything beyond the tinsel surface. A hero is a hero for the right reasons, and has shown that a human being is capable of more than most of us will ever achieve. A hero displays bravery, and heroes will often risk their lives for others. Their stories will live on for generations. The Messiah who was longed for by the Jews was to be their hero.

Contemplate what makes Jesus more than just our hero. His birth and baptism were accompanied by extraordinary signs of angels, stars and doves, but this is not some publicity stunt by God the Father. Our Saviour Jesus' life and death and resurrection would not just save the few that he came into contact with in his earthly life, but changed the whole history of humankind, and will go on changing it for ever.

As you desire to imitate him

Saviour of us all, may this world again
Be surprised and transformed by the vision
Of heaven opening. May the coming of the Holy Spirit
So bless your Church that it works for your glory;
For you long to be pleased with your people.
Amen.

The Second Sunday of Epiphany

John 2.1–11

Gaze on all the colours of this occasion . . . See the vibrant wedding robes; the table piled high with rich food, the pink of pomegranates, the shock of oranges, the purples of the grapes, the sheen of the olives. The excitement mounts. Hear the pipes and horns and drums of the band as the bride is ushered in.

Are you one of the guests, who have just heard a whispered rumour that the wine's run out? What an insult! Are you the bridegroom who can't bear the disgrace? Are you the steward who fears for his job when it's found out how he miscalculated? Are you Mary, concerned for her friends, but sure that her extraordinary son can avert disaster?

Consider all the changes taking place in this story. A wedding is not just a party, it is a time when a woman is changed into a wife, and a man into a husband and, with these new titles, comes a new vocation, to live for each other. Then there is Mary, who has changed, from the young girl who received a birth and a great commission, into a mother. And possibly now a widow. The Gospel describes her as Jesus' mother, but Jesus calls her 'dear woman': Mary must let him go as her child. But she does not disappear from the story. Though we never hear her speak again, she is a constant presence, changed into one of his most faithful disciples. She has a new vocation, and moves into a new stage of her life, just as Jesus is changing from the local hero into the public figure and taking on the responsibility of the Word within him. And finally, of course, there is the change of the water into wine, showing us God's generous love; when you've had enough of what you think you want, God gives what he wants to give, what he knows is now right and best for you.

Contemplate where in your life you long for water to be turned into wine. Who are the people you pray for who need to have hope in difficult circumstances? Where in your life are relationships jaded or plans stalled? Jesus can transform these if we only ask.

As we grow older we are prone to lose our youthful optimism and we are tempted to believe that the good times are over. We must remember the words of the steward, 'You have saved the best till now.' Let us be alert to such opportunities.

As you desire to imitate him

Unchanging God, make me open to change
And prepared for challenge.
Your love brings hope from despair
And joy from disaster;
As I grow through all the stages of my life,
May my vocation grow too, and never waver.
Amen.

The Third Sunday of Epiphany

Luke 4.14–21

Gaze on the scene in the synagogue. The men crowd in, some who normally wouldn't bother to attend, but today have rediscovered their piety in the urge to see what the fuss is about. They arrive early so they'll get a seat with a view. The rich and elders have their own personal seats and come in at the last minute, alarmed at the excitement that disturbs their usual devotions. Here come the young men, too, the ones who've grown up with Jesus, and went to study the Scriptures with him. They can't believe he's special. Yes, he knew his Bible back to front, but wasn't he the boring one that actually took the classes seriously? Hardly someone to hang about with.

In the side gallery the women whisper and press their noses to the grill to get a glimpse. Their children cling to their skirts and tease each other.

Mary arrives and they make room for her. She sits down, nervously.

Consider the passage Jesus chose, one they were all familiar with. If the reading was a surprise, consider what Jesus says next. His sermon must count as the shortest in history! No one expected anything as dramatic as this: 'Today this scripture is fulfilled in your hearing.'

Consider all the key moments of Jewish history that this passage alludes to, for Jesus is echoing Isaiah, who in turn is referring to the Babylonian captivity but also harking back to the exodus of the slaves from Egypt. It's almost like a corridor of mirrors, where the view is for ever receding but replicating. All those listening would have understood these allusions, and grasped that the 'year of the Lord's favour' meant the day of salvation as well as the year of the Jubilee, when all debts were to be annulled. And so those present who were radical, politically minded opponents of the Roman occupation would have seized upon these words and seen in Jesus someone to lead them in the fight. Galilee was famous for its rebels; was Jesus just another one, or would he turn out to be the one who would change things so much that after him no other rebel would be needed?

Contemplate the silence after Jesus sat down.

Contemplate the simplicity of what he has said. He is not inventing a new theology or elaborating a complicated strategy. Let us take Jesus at face value for once as these words speak to us and tell us where our priorities must lie. He has come among us to announce, to release, to recover and to free.

As you desire to imitate him

Sovereign Lord, give me the courage
To stand up and announce your word
In my workplace, and in my street,
To those I don't know, and to those who know me.
Even if I feel embarrassed and uncertain,
Give me strength to preach and proclaim,
To heal and to free the poor and oppressed.
Amen.

The Fourth Sunday of Epiphany

Luke 2.22–40

Gaze on a diamond just mined from deep underground, formed from elements from the beginning of time. It is dull until it's been polished, and only the expert knows what is to be looked for. Another diamond is discovered in a river bed, exposed by torrents, appearing innocuously as an exceptionally hard, white pebble. But where the outer layer has rubbed thin, there is the promise of something miraculous. Once in the hands of the jeweller, it will be liberated to reveal its love affair with the light, able to play with the beams of the sun and set off a symphony of colour, flashing as if burning with fire.

Consider the various meanings of the word *reveal*. On a simple level it means to allow something once out of sight to appear. The word is not far from its root 'veil'; so the bride lifts her veil to reveal her face at the wedding, or the curtain is drawn back to display a new portrait of the Queen. More abstractly, we use the word when we talk of disclosing knowledge – how scientists reveal the secrets of the universe, and underwater photography reveals the beauty of the hidden world on the seabed. And then we come to the religious meaning, whereby a truth is revealed by inspiration, or supernatural means, so that our faith is called a revealed religion, because we would not have understood God's ways unless he'd chosen to reveal them to us.

Examine this passage for the repeated clues to the importance of looking and seeing the signs, as a way not only of revealing the future, but the hearts of each one of us.

For the revelation we are seeing in the thanksgiving of Simeon and Anna is a mixture of all these meanings. Simeon tells us that he has been inspired to expect this child, but also that his own eyes are recognizing the promised salvation, as if a veil has fallen and baby Jesus is revealed in his full maturity. Both these witnesses disclose a knowledge that they have discerned by the depth of their watchfulness and prayerfulness. Revelation cannot take place in the dark.

Consider Simeon's next step, taking the idea even further, that this revelation is not personal to him, or reserved for his people, the Israel of the Temple, but is also to be a light to the Gentiles.

Contemplate the children in your life – cousins or younger brothers, children or neighbours' children, grandchildren, or god-daughters, and how as they grow they reveal their personality in small, slow ways. Contemplate how children grow from physical helplessness, when they rely on others for everything, to independence and an ability to take care of themselves. At the same time their minds also grow away from childish fancies to an adult understanding. We need to be sound in body and mind to be fully human. So verse 40 should not be overlooked as an afterthought, but seen as an important reminder to us of our responsibilities for all the children we nurture.

As you desire to imitate him

Sovereign Lord, may I watch and pray with patience
And see the signs around me
And discern your thoughts within me.
I ask that the Holy Spirit be upon me,
So that I may reveal your glory to the world
And shine with your salvation.
Amen.

ORDINARY TIME

Proper 1

------◆------

Luke 5.1–11

Gaze on a shoal of fish. Imagine the weight of herring that used to be caught in the nets of the North Sea trawlers. Nets that have been torn at sea and mended countless times by patient, rough hands. The fish shine in the sunlight as they wriggle on deck. They are like a hoard of silver coins or a sudden shower of rain. The fishermen cannot control the size of their catch, only rely on their experience to know where they might go for the best chance to succeed.

In this story, Simon and his mates have been out all night and despite their best endeavours, have returned empty-handed. Share their despondency and worry – another few nights like this and their livelihood will be threatened.

Consider how well these disciples must have known Jesus by now, for they did just what he suggested, however bizarre it seemed, and however open to ridicule this made them among their fellow fishermen. Jesus had been in their town for a little while and had already begun to heal and preach. So Simon was impressed enough with Jesus to call him 'Master'. Jesus hadn't just chosen Simon out of the blue – he must have observed him before and made his choice. This growing relationship was one of mutual discovery. Yet Jesus was a carpenter, not a fisherman. What did he know of the mysteries of the life that teemed beneath the waves?

Consider how, once the disciples had obeyed him, they were so convinced by this event that they left everything to follow him. Perhaps it was because he met them in their real need. He didn't perform some flash miracle that left their lives unchanged. This miracle was Jesus meeting them in their world, and proving to them that his Good News was particular and specific to them, tailored to their situation and capable of turning round their lives. And that is what Jesus will do for each of us if we trust him enough. For he called the men by name.

Contemplate putting out into deep water. We cannot serve Jesus or catch people for him by staying in the safe shallows. We must risk danger and storm; ridicule and disappointment.

But not necessarily alone, for Jesus expected his disciples to work as a team. Fishermen above all others trust their lives to the skill of their crew. Jesus does not ask us to work for him in isolation. With others to support us, we will find the task less daunting. Contemplate who are the allies that you can work with today.

As you desire to imitate him

Dear Jesus, may I hear your call
And learn to be prepared to put out into deep water
To carry out your will.
Bless all missionaries and evangelists:
May your Holy Spirit inspire them
with the words and skills to act in your name.
Amen.

Proper 2

———◆———

Luke 6.17–26

Gaze on the waiting room in a busy hospital. Pale walls bear replica Monets and dull still lifes of sallow fruit, and these are meant to calm you somehow. Lino echoes with each nurse's step. People sit around, some chatting quietly, others gaze ahead, each person hiding their worry and symptoms. The elderly are brought in wheelchairs, and small children wriggle on their mothers' laps. The patient experiences total helplessness. There will be talk and tests, and prodding and injections, results and maybe, at last, a diagnosis, followed by prescriptions and medications and operations. But what people remember most after a spell in hospital is the kind word from the nursing auxiliary, the flowers sent from a sister who lives too far away to visit, or the hand held by the chaplain.

Consider Jesus' compassion for the needy in all their lack – lack of health, wealth, food or power, and even joy. After giving them a physical healing, he leaves them something more precious – hope, and a vision of an order of society where there would be no more oppression, physical or spiritual. Though he healed all who were there, he knew there would always be more. So he is moved to disclose the truths behind the sufferings of the world, and the depths of God's ways. First he starts with a hope, and reveals the promise in God's law, just as we heard it in Mary's great song (Luke 1.51–53).

Consider how Luke's version of the Sermon puts them all in a 'level place'. It is as well, for he then moves from consolation to the opposite, and brings us all down to earth with a bump. For after the blessings, he turns them upside down and prophesies the woes that wait for the rich, the well fed, those who laugh, and are well regarded.

Consider which category the vast majority of us reading these blessings and woes today fall into. We can persuade ourselves that Jesus means his descriptions to be spiritual, but reading this, it seems remarkably clear that he also meant it to be taken literally. The Jews of his time knew from their Scripture that the poor should be protected; but for the rich to be threatened this way was a further idea that would have punctured their self-satisfaction, and should puncture ours.

Contemplate Jesus' advice to us to 'rejoice' in the day when we are hated, excluded and insulted, and rejected because of him. What a giant thing it is that Jesus asks of us! Contemplate how it is that people who endure suffering with love and hope intact, and survive persecution with dignity and forgiveness in their hearts, are ultimately free in a way that their persecutors never will be.

As you desire to imitate him

Healing Lord, touch me with your power
And reveal to me the true blessings of your Kingdom.
May I shun the woe in store for the self-satisfied
Who do not depend on you.
Help me rather to find riches in leading a humble life.
Amen.

Proper 3

———◆◆◆———

Luke 6.27–38

Gaze on a traffic jam and imagine yourself behind the wheel, smelling the fumes of the cars all around, and hearing the bass beat of a loud radio. You're on the main road into town, but there's a side road that joins in at such an angle that the traffic from the left keeps filtering in ahead of you. The clock ticks by and your stream of cars is hardly moving. You'll be late for work again; you sit and fret. As the irritation rises within you, you cast around for someone to blame. You rail against the unfairness of the situation, the road design, and the stupidity of the drivers ahead that let the others in. Why should they allow the interlopers preference? You long to get out, knock on their windows, and tell them to get a move on! Road rage is so near the surface for us all.

Consider what a dangerous mix it is when the bile of impatience collides with our sense of being wronged. Surely the Christian way is not to mind, to allow others to go first, to put their needs before yours. Dilemmas like the one above seem trivial, but are the daily, uninspiring challenges of being a Christian. We rarely connect the routine impatience or minor protest with Jesus' call to us to turn the other cheek or share our cloak. It seems as if God is asking too much of us in this passage. If we are sensible, why should we defer to those who are less so? If we are caring, why should we suffer at the hands of the careless? How difficult it is to see the thoughtless driver as our neighbour, and we certainly don't see the relevance of Jesus' words to the Highway Code!

Consider a further challenge – how many of us would give back what we never stole (Psalm 69.4)? Or as it might be in everyday life, must you pick up the litter which someone else dropped, or wash up the dishes you never dirtied? For at the root of all these silly examples is the biggest question of all: how much are you willing to forgive? We are frightened to start down this road of extravagance, because we fear where it might lead; it might lead to a cross. But if we cannot succeed in being Christlike in the little things of life, how likely is it that when the moment a great sacrifice is demanded, we will be ready to stand up for our Lord?

Contemplate these words of St Francis of Assisi: 'The servant of God cannot know how much patience and humility he has within himself as long as everything goes well with him. But when the time comes in which those who should do him justice do quite the opposite to him, he has only as much patience and humility as he has on that occasion, and not more.' (St Francis, Admonitions)

Contemplate the last time this applied to you.

As you desire to imitate him

Most High Father, you call on me to copy your Son
And be merciful in my dealings with those who wrong or
　　slight me.
May I lend my time and talents, my wealth and my
　　possessions,
Without expectation of return or reward,
For nothing I have is mine to keep
Except for your love and forgiveness.
Amen.

The Second Sunday before Lent

Luke 8.22–25

Gaze on all the storms and flooding that towns and villages have suffered in Britain in recent years. Remember how violently the water rushed, stronger than a battering-ram, breaking down river banks and inundating the streets and homes. Look inside the privacy of a once comfortable home, at carpets patterned with mud, wallpaper lined with mould, and chairs piled up on tables. Gaze on the pictures of people in other countries, suffering from mud slides that bury whole villages. Gaze on the people of Bangladesh who wade up to their necks in water to reach safety. Listen to the power of the waves as they break along the shore, louder than any cannon.

Consider what this question means – 'Where is your faith?' Does it mean where have you hidden it, or have you left it behind like a bag on the bus? Or, why has it been lost, like water draining fast away? Or does it mean – where does your faith come from? Does it come from your senses – the human touch that brings connection and comfort, or the sounds of Bach and Handel that stir the spirit, or the Sunday hymns that swell and escape the church of brick and stone? Does faith dwell in our minds, which wrestle with questions of why and how and scientific proof? Or does it come from the power of Jesus' presence and from careful consideration of his authority? Do you place faith in that revolution of thought and action which our Lord prescribed as the only salvation for this world? Faith must be the hope that God is the invisible but strong bond that links together all the stories of our lives and weaves them into the greater story of creation and the universe. Faith, that one small boat on a storm-tossed ocean, is as visible to God as a galaxy of suns and stars. We must hold together the seeming contradiction that though we are not the centre of the universe, God's purposes for us will prevail 'as the waters cover the sea'.

Contemplate where your faith is when, like the disciples, you are adrift in a storm. Contemplate the times in the past when faith has been challenged by personal loss and grief, by disappointment or hurt caused by others. Can you still trust that the Lord is with you in this storm-tossed boat we all share?

Contemplate where your faith is when life is going well – is it still central, or do you rely on your own strength, and fail to acknowledge the source of all good?

As you desire to imitate him

Dear Lord, I cannot imitate your command of the winds and
    the waves;
I know my place in the natural world is insignificant
But your incarnation makes me count somehow.
May I place my faith in your love and power
So that when I am in danger, I pray rather than panic
And when life is good, I give thanks.
Amen.

The Sunday next before Lent

Luke 9.28–36 [37–43a]

Gaze on all things that dazzle – spume of the waves that roam the sea, and is tossed up like tinsel in the air, or the light on a lake, making silver rays skid over the surface like a thousand steel skates flashing across ice. Gaze on the astonishment of snow that brightens the dullness of winter days, and transforms the well-known landscape into a quite different scene. But beware, because if you stare too long at snow it can cause blindness. Gaze on lightening, never still, always restless, always questing a way back to earth. All these examples of blinding light have one thing in common, for though you know the real world is still there, everything seems changed. 'For beauty's nothing/but beginning of Terror we're still just able to bear' (Rainer Maria Rilke).

Consider how the scene of the Transfiguration follows in Luke straight after the great moment when Peter names Jesus as the Christ. He is quite clear in his mind that Jesus is not Elijah or any of the other old prophets, 'come back to life' (v. 19). Yet here are the prophets appearing, as heralds, or witnesses, or perhaps as worshippers.

Consider what a conversation between Moses, Elijah and Jesus could possibly be like. What would Hero, Prophet and Lord of All share? Would they be regretting the fallibility of humanity, and sighing over all the wrong turnings we've taken, and the advice unheeded? Just like a teacher and a parent talking together on Parents' Evening: 'I've already told her that a hundred times', the parent says despairingly of the wayward child. Would Moses and Elijah try to warn Jesus – 'They won't listen to you either?' Or would they have confirmed his destiny, and encouraged him not to turn back?

Consider how God has signposted himself for us through many people, at many times, and will do so now. The Transfiguration is the supreme moment when God blessed Peter and John and James with confirmation upon confirmation. All of us who have ever prayed 'Lord, give me a sign' must envy these three.

Contemplate the cloud that came and overshadowed the disciples, after the dazzling light. Let your heart enter deep into that cloud. The nameless mystic who wrote *The Cloud of Unknowing* in the fourteenth century understood very well the paradox of prayer:

> Therefore I will leave on one side everything I can think, and choose for my love that thing which I cannot think. Why? Because he may well be loved, but not thought. By love he can be caught and held, but by thinking never . . . And you are to . . . try to penetrate the darkness above you. Strike that thick cloud of unknowing with the sharp dart of longing love, and on no account think of giving up.

As you desire to imitate him

Transfigured Lord, may I listen to your truth spoken by the
    prophets;
May I hear your voice calling me,
Affirming me as your child,
And may I reverence you in awe
And sometimes shine with your glory.
Amen.

LENT

The First Sunday of Lent

Luke 4.1–13

Gaze on Jesus in the wilderness. Gaze on the harsh monochrome of fear and confusion, on the hard bed of stones that brings no comfort. Imagine forty days without the scent of grass, his feet cut raw against the ragged paths, as he searches for water and is driven to lick dew from the rocks. He is counting the days by the size of the moon, dazed by the infinity of night, an indigo canvas pricked by silver stars that stretches for ever and never reaches an answer. His mouth has grown foul, and his breath stinks for there has been no chance to wash for weeks. There is grit beneath his nails, he digs holes for his excrement, and wipes himself half clean with torn leaves.

And here you are, wrapped in your warm duvet, while Jesus' teeth chatter as he rolls himself in his cloak.

Consider the Lenten fast that Jesus underwent; then consider what you have decided to 'give up' for Lent. The comparison is shaming, is it not? Becoming more disciplined by learning to do without some of our luxuries is not a bad exercise. Indeed it is one we should follow all year round. But it should not be compared in the same breath with the deprivations Jesus accepted while in the wilderness. Jesus showed us that there is no living without pain, that prayer can be a bitter struggle and decision making can become a nightmare of temptation.

Consider what a difference it would make in our lives if we resisted the temptations that faced Jesus – the temptation to easy power, the temptation for easy living, the temptation to easy fame. Consider how easy your life is, and how rarely if given the choice you accept the more difficult route, the harder task, the more uncomfortable action.

Consider how you make decisions in your life. When faced with tempting possibilities, how often do you reach for the Bible to give you help and advice? Do you know your Bible well enough for answers to spring readily to mind? For all Jesus' replies to the devil are direct quotes from Deuteronomy. Jesus was so steeped in his faith, and so educated in his religion, that he had swift access to the wisdom of their words. Like anti-biotics which fight the bacteria in our body, they were his defence against evil.

Contemplate what you can do this Lent to really identify with Jesus' exile in the wilderness. Contemplate what you can sacrifice to simplify your standard of living. Contemplate what you can study, so that you will be as able as Jesus was to use Scripture to withstand temptation.

As you desire to imitate him

Lord God, my protector,
So fill me with your holy Spirit
And guard me with your word,
That through the arid times of my prayer life
And the desolate periods of my existence
I may withstand temptation
And be rewarded with fresh hope.
Amen.

The Second Sunday of Lent

———•◆•———

Luke 13.31–35

Gaze on Jerusalem today, in greater need than ever of her children being gathered together in harmony. It is a city divided between Jew and Muslim, Jew and Christian, with no-go areas armed by guns. Churches are locked. Doubt and suspicion poison all communication and relationships. Many areas are desolate and abandoned, as settlements encroach and livelihoods are displaced.

See the Al Aqsa Mosque rising and shining above the city, so beautifully. At its heart is Abraham's footprint – Abraham, with whom God made a covenant that he should become the founder of a great nation, now a divided people. And skirting one side, the Western Wall, its hallowed bricks carrying the paper prayers of countless Jews.

Consider the false concern of the Pharisees, designed to trick Jesus: either give up, or press on to confrontation with the representatives of power in the world; the very power he rejected in the temptations. Consider why it is that Jerusalem (and for Jerusalem, we can substitute any great power – Washington, London, Moscow) kills the prophets sent to it. Why does the established order find it so difficult to listen to challenges and consider change? People with influence do not ever want to give it up. And we should include in this group all of us in the comfortable West who have a vested interest in sustaining our economy and security and in maintaining borders. They – we – are hugely defensive of our current status and fear

44

anything that might reduce our ability to control events. We resist sharing with outsiders. Just think about how rife 'Nimbyism' is, even among groups who are of similar backgrounds and heritage. 'Go and try out your experiment for sacrificial sharing and community somewhere else; but not here', we say, when they plan a hostel for the mentally ill in our street. And so when a prophet comes among us, we reject his or her word: it can't be meant for us, and if they persist they must be silenced – today not by stoning, but by ridicule or, more often, we just ignore them.

Contemplate Jesus' steadfastness. He will not be deflected from his goal. Jesus talks here of a practical journey he is making to Jerusalem, but this also symbolizes his whole ministry. He will continue his good work of preaching and performing cures and yet Herod wants to kill him. Jesus will complete his vision – 'I must keep going' – not escaping from danger, but travelling towards it.

Contemplate how sure you are of your goal in life, and how committed you are to reaching it, and how strong you are to withstand those who would have you give up.

As you desire to imitate him

Steadfast Lord, may I keep going till my goal is reached.
Make me willing to be gathered by you
With those I barely tolerate,
Those who make me uneasy
And those who threaten me,
Into the unity of your spirit.
Amen.

The Third Sunday of Lent

---·•·•·---

Luke 13.1–9

Gaze on the villagers, clustered on a street corner, or heads together on the synagogue steps, appalled at the latest news. The story of the defilement and murder of their fellow countrymen at the hands of Pilate must have terrified them. How they longed for rescue from this tyrant, and the rule of Rome. Then someone else says, 'Yes, that's bad enough, but have you heard – those workers on the Siloam Tower, all dead! Those jerry-builders have a lot to answer for.' Then another man who'd been listening quietly pipes up: 'There must be more to it than that. They must have brought it on themselves; there can't be any other explanation for such a tragedy.' As they strive for an answer, here comes Jesus, who is so respected for his wisdom and teaching. Surely he will have the answer. Hear them asking Jesus, was this violence a punishment for their sins? Where is the justice in this otherwise?

Consider Jesus' reply, giving us the hard truth we know in our bones but fight against all our lives: bad things can happen to good people, and God's love and power will not protect us. There was nothing predestined or deserving about their fate. How common such catastrophes must have been in an age when the lives of workers were cheap and 'health and safety' unheard of. When we hear of the suffering of someone we love, we'll surely say, 'But they don't deserve that.' When we hear of the suffering of those we disapprove of, some corner of our hearts thinks, 'They got what was coming to them.' But Jesus goes further, and uses this news to make a different point. Are we so sure we are good people? Aren't we all sinners in need of repentance? So do not judge these unfortunates who suffered violent deaths, for none of us knows the date of our death. Beware feeling smug; judge yourself, for none of us are entirely innocent. Consider this passage with last week's, which also prophesied doom for the people. Together, they emphasize the threat that Jesus predicted, and the urgency of repentance.

Contemplate the parable Jesus gives us of the fig tree, which hides a serious, even frightening message. The fig tree is us, as individuals or maybe as a society, or a nation. What good are we doing? Are we bearing fruit and growing in grace?

God is patient and will wait; he will give us second, third and fourth chances to repent and reform. But at some point, his mercy will be balanced by judgement. The justice we seek here on earth does exist in God's scheme of things, and we are as vulnerable to it as others.

As you desire to imitate him

Dear Lord and Judge, may I use this Lent
To throw myself on your mercy
Before it is too late.
Help me to examine my soul
And repent, that I may not perish,
But grow, and bear fruit.
Amen.

The Fourth Sunday of Lent

Luke 15.1–3, 11b–32

Gaze on the father pacing his lemon groves each evening, climbing to the highest point of his land to scan the horizon. And at last he sees a dot, growing ever more distinct, ever more familiar.

Gaze on the elder son, the outsider looking in at the party, sulking and aggrieved. Nothing tastes sweet to him any more, not even his mother's honey cakes which she tempts him with. (Where *is* the mother in this story?) His mouth is dry and has a permanent taste of winter olives. He is not the first brother in the Bible to have fallen out with his sibling. First Cain killed Abel; next Jacob stole his heritage from Esau. Then Jacob's sons attempted murder, all because of a coat. This elder son didn't have to stain his hands with fraud or slaughter, for the younger son had left of his own accord. Good riddance.

Consider how the power of this story is magnified by its place in the lectionary sequence, after three weeks of dire prophecy and grim warnings of death and destruction, and just before the crucifixion, the worst story of all.

Consider next its particular place in Luke, after two stories of the lost sheep and coin (which we will return to later this year). But if this is only the third of a set, it could have finished at v. 24, when the son returns and the festivities begin. So what else does Jesus want to show us? This is the second reading in a row to struggle with our deep confusion about the unfairness of life. From the elder son's point of view, he has much to be offended by. Put yourself in his plodding, never-a-foot-wrong shoes. Most of us are the elder son and have to be taught the lesson of humility, and the wrongness of passing judgements which are not ours to pass. For it is the elder son who excludes himself from the party and descends into a hell of isolation.

Finally, consider the common title of this story, taken from the King James translation: 'The Prodigal Son'. Look up the meaning of prodigal and you find 'reckless', 'wasteful', 'lavish'. In which case, this story should be called the Parable of the Prodigal Father, for that is exactly how God the Father dispenses his love.

Contemplate the key moment in this story, which categorically defines the loving nature of our God: 'while he [the erring son] was still a long way off, his father saw him' and he ran to meet him (v. 20). Just as this father opened wide his arms to embrace his lost son, soon we will see God in the Son love us so much he will open wide his arms on the cross.

As you desire to imitate him

Compassionate Father, I thank you for your lavish love.
I have sinned against heaven and against you:
I rejected you and you let me go,
I stayed away and you mourned,
I came to my senses and you embraced me;
I repented and you restored me
Through the death and resurrection of your Son,
Our Lord Jesus Christ.
Amen.

The Fifth Sunday of Lent

John 12.1–8

Gaze on this cosy domestic setting, spruced up for a special celebration. It seems that this house is the nearest Jesus came to an adult family home. Martha is being Martha again – the carer in the kitchen. Mary is being Mary as ever – impetuous dreamer, passionate in her affection, her admiration bordering on worship. Perhaps her heart is overwhelmed still with gratitude for the restoration of their brother Lazarus to them, and she seeks the most extravagant way of saying thank you.

Smell all the fragrances that bring beauty into our lives: the first cut of grass in the spring; the scent of roses after rain; your baby at bath time. Now, the small, humble room in Bethany explodes with this perfect perfume. Smell the fragrance of the nard, distilled from valerian, gathered in the northern mountains of Europe and imported to the East. No wonder it was so costly.

Consider how Mary's pouring out of the ointment stands for so much more; it is the pouring out of all she values most. Why do we save our treasures up for special moments, keeping them in the back of the cupboard, never quite sure the occasion merits the best champagne? Why do we not rather turn the ordinary moment into something special by gracing it with delight? For we don't know when it may be too late.

Mary knew instinctively what Paul explains in today's epistle: 'for whose sake I have lost all things . . . that I may gain Christ' (Philippians 3.7–14).

Today is the beginning of Passiontide and Mary's passionate action is remarkable, quite 'over the top'. Not only does she wash Jesus' feet, she wipes them with her hair. Did her spontaneous demonstration of love come to Jesus' mind later that week, in the Upper Room, and spur him on to wash the feet of his disciples?

Contemplate the passionate love of God in creating the world, his passion in forgiving our blindness and wickedness, and the passion that led him to risk so much and send his Son. Contemplate what you feel passionate about. What would make you risk so much or give away so much? Many of us have a reserved nature, and are not much given to grand or passionate gestures. But contemplate the martyrs and missionaries who gave up everything to gain Christ. What makes them so very different from most of us?

As you desire to imitate him

Dear Lord, as we approach Holy Week
May I imitate Mary: I will kneel at your feet
And worship you with all the best of me.
I will walk with you to the Cross
And be prepared to suffer with you.
I will keep vigil at the tomb and rise with you.
So shall my loss be gain
And my tears be turned into joy.
Amen.

Palm Sunday
The Liturgy of the Palms

---•◆•◆•---

Luke 19.28–40

Gaze on that onlooker at the back, peering over the taller people at the front of the crowds. It could be you or me. Your heart is thumping, you are so exhilarated. For once, feel ready to come out of your safe corner and move towards centre stage and stand in the glare of the limelight. Be in the thick of it, waving ecstatically, grabbing whatever will act as a flag, waving it to reach nearer to heaven. You're clapping in time to the clop of the donkey's hooves. Everyone's spirits are surging. Be part of a great collective 'yes'. Gaze on hope personified, riding on the donkey's back. In this moment the past is dismissed, the future only gain. Feel the joy of this crowd.

Consider what can change in so short a week. 'A week is a long time in politics' they say, and make no mistake, Jesus had thrust himself into the centre of politics with a vengeance, the politics of church and state, of leaders and led, of imperialists and subjugated. And yet he is rewriting all the religious politics of his day, and dividing his people in the process.

Consider: if only the crowd had kept faith with this vision of freedom – but sometimes freedom is just what we fear most. If only they had applauded him in the Temple as much as they did in the streets. If only they had driven back the soldiers from Gethsemane and cried 'Shame on you' to Judas. If only they had called out 'Jesus' instead of that fatal shout 'Barabbas'. The same crowd that greeted him on Palm Sunday was later

whipped up by different emotions and turned into a dangerous mob. Consider how many chances they – we – the ordinary
people – had to save Jesus, so many opportunities to stand
shoulder to shoulder and declare him the true King of the Jews.
United like that, would Pilate have dared or Caiaphas been so
emboldened or Herod empowered to condemn him?

Consider how dreadful is our vacillation, our reticence, our
fickleness. For that is all it takes to turn away from the Father,
to betray the Son, and all it takes to snuff out the flame of the
Spirit.

Contemplate 'if they keep quiet, the stones will cry out': contemplate the relationship Jesus had with the natural world, his
authority over waves and bread, and broken bones and water,
all of which he could transform through the Creator's power.
Contemplate why the Creator God is silent in Holy Week, until
the moment of the crucifixion when darkness came over the
whole land.

As you desire to imitate him

Dear Lord, let my worship of you
Last beyond Palm Sunday.
May I remain faithful with you
    Through the confusion of Gethsemane,
    The injustice of the trial
    And the cruelty of the crucifixion.
Let me not turn away
Nor through cowardice abandon you,
My King and my Redeemer.
Amen.

EASTER

Easter Day

Luke 24.1–12

Gaze on the early dawn. Each time we see it, it is as if we live through all the stages of creation again. First all is chaos and confusion, the stars are obscured by cloud and so is the moon. One moment nothing is visible, all is dark and we stumble about, time unknowable, earth and sky one hopeless muddle, the world empty and formless. Then shapes begin to appear, trees and buildings loom grey and insubstantial. Distances don't make sense until the sky lightens a little more and there is a streak, sometimes violent as fire, sometimes smooth as silk and gentle as pearl, dividing the sky from the earth. Gaze on the day beginning again, making visible what never went away. Hear the first bird sing.

Consider what a stone rolled away would say to you – thieves perhaps, or soldiers acting on Pilate's orders, checking up that he's really dead? Consider what an empty tomb would tell you – the body gone, stolen perhaps? Consider what two men in dazzling clothes would tell you. Are these angels, spirits, or ghosts? Am I dreaming or am I mad? The truth never dawns, the messengers must spell it out. Do you believe now? Certainly the Apostles did not – why believe the idle tale of over-emotional women? But still, the stone moved, the body gone – the women excited: surely they ought to check. Would you?

Consider what is the abiding feature of Jesus' resurrection body: it is not just that he is visible, but that he is *present*.

Consider how this presence is more powerful than just a visible ghost would be. Even when your back is turned, the presence of someone you love fills the room, and strengthens you. And this presence is not just a one-to-one individual experience. Jesus returned to a group for the purpose of galvanizing a community. And though he is no longer still visible to us, his *presence* is very real when two or three gather together. The importance of the community of Christians should not be underestimated.

Contemplate the times in your life when God has rolled away the stone that has trapped you in the dark, without any hope. Give thanks for the release he brought you. Or pray for resurrection hope, if now is a time when you feel buried by pain or grief, shame or despair.

Contemplate the mystery of Jesus escaping from death. His escape releases us from the limitations of mortality. This is the greatest reversal of them all.

As you desire to imitate him

Risen Jesus, may I imitate the women
In the persistence of their love
And the dedication of their service,
Even when they believed you dead.
May I take my place in the community
Of those who know your presence,
And today of all days, give thanks
That your love for us cannot be quenched.
Amen.

The Second Sunday of Easter

---·•·---

John 20.19–31

Gaze on the faces of the disciples, their jaws clenched, eyes half shut, pictures of defeat. So far we have been gazing on expressions of fright and grief, of doubt and confusion. They've seen the stone rolled away, and they've seen the empty tomb, and they've heard the women's 'idle tale'. Can anything more happen to astonish them?

Gaze on this huddle of frightened men and women whispering in the dark, behind a shut and bolted door. Listen to the silence; there is no creak of a footstep on the stairs or whine of hinges as a door swings open.

Now gaze at Jesus, standing there, the dark room flooded with light. Hear his voice speak the word 'Shalom'. See his terrible wounds.

Gaze at the disciples again; at last, see joy on their faces.

Consider dear Thomas, so much maligned down the centuries. He was only asking of Jesus what the other disciples had already been granted – to see that this Jesus is more than an apparition. Consider Jesus saying those words, meant for us today: 'Blessed are those who have not seen yet have believed.' We have the harder task, for we must place our faith in the honesty and sense of ordinary men and women who lived 2000 years ago and carried these stories in their hearts until the time came to write them down. Consider the nature of belief and the dismal gap between what we believe in our heads and what we know in our hearts. Not until head and heart combine can our will carry out God's law of love.

Consider how important it is to know that this Jesus standing there carries into the Kingdom the marks of the nails. By this, God shows us that pain and suffering are not wiped away, but can be transformed. Though we must not ask for our griefs to be as if they never were, we can be confident that we will move beyond our suffering. We carry the scars because it is the scars which make us who we are.

Contemplate the varieties of peace that belief in the risen Jesus brings – peace from fear of human frailty, and peace of certainty, banishing confusion and chaos; the peace of serenity in the face of grief, that knows the power of suffering will not rule supreme; and peace that we rest in the eternal love of God. These are all positive peace, that give us strength.

As you desire to imitate him

Grant me, risen Lord, trust in your resurrection.
So inspire me with the breath of your Spirit,
So bless me with your peace,
That my fear is transformed to joy,
A joy that invites others to listen, look and believe.
Amen.

The Third Sunday of Easter

John 21.1–19

Gaze on another dawn, another occasion when at first all is in shadow until Jesus illuminates the day for the disciples. Gaze on another setting when things are going badly: if there are no fish, at best the disciples won't eat, and at worst there will be nothing to sell at market, no means of earning a living. Gaze and see how Jesus brings success out of failure.

Feel the cool breeze from the sea and warm your hands by the fire. Gaze on yet another meal shared with Jesus; though not a banquet, this one is prepared by him, and is as welcome as it is surprising. Did the disciples eat in silence, staring at the Lord, or were they by now comfortable with his resurrected presence, able to treat him as their old friend, chatting away, plying him with questions and bringing him up to date with the news?

Consider the details that make this story so believable. The teller remembers that before Peter leaps into the sea 'he wrapped his outer garment around him (for he had taken it off)'. And later we are allowed to share Peter's innermost feelings for he 'was hurt'. Such descriptions convince us that we are hearing the very echo of Peter relating this story, some years after the event. This must be the authentic voice of Peter.

Consider the length of this story. Or rather, these two stories. The first is about the fishing expedition and the beach breakfast, which is in fact a simple eucharist – Jesus came, took bread and gave it to them. The second is about the conversation between

60

Jesus and Peter. What connects the two halves are the words of the disciples to Peter, 'We'll go with you' (v. 3), mirrored at the end by Jesus telling him he will end his life going 'where you do not wish to go' (v. 18). For our faith is a journey not always of our own choosing. Consider what this tells us Christians – that we must be prepared for change and development. Christian faith does not allow you to stay safe on the shore, and here Jesus warns Peter just that. His future will be full of risk.

Consider also how the disciples knew it was Jesus in this familiar miracle – surely it was by abundance brought out of scarcity, and lack turned into plenty. The net was not torn, because Jesus can shower us with gifts till we think our arms can't carry any more, but still there's more to come.

Contemplate Jesus calling you by your name. Maybe your first name or your nickname. He is talking straight to your secret self. For he reverts to calling Peter 'Simon', going back to the man he first met, before Peter betrayed him at the trial. Somehow Simon must be transformed once more back into Peter, the Rock.

Contemplate God's great mercy in giving Simon the chance to wipe out the shame of his threefold denial. Contemplate the mercy God might similarly have shown Judas, if his shame had not driven him to suicide.

As you desire to imitate him

Forgiving Lord, may I grow to love you
With the certainty of Peter.
And with the courage that this love brings
May I be willing to go where I may not wish to go,
To feed your sheep and care for your people,
And face the consequences
In the strength of your Spirit.
Amen.

The Fourth Sunday of Easter

---◆---

John 10.22–30

Gaze on a rough, stormy day in Jerusalem. Our usual picture of the Holy Land is of sun and heat, and a life led in the open air, but there can be cold winds and rain, too. Jesus is sheltering in one of the inner courts of the Temple. It's not just the weather that's turned stormy, for now he's trapped, encircled by a group of opponents who harangue and taunt him, willing him on to blaspheme. This is an unofficial trial. Hear the spite in their voices, crackling like kindling on a fire, their threats spitting like water splashed in oil. Gaze on Jesus, standing his ground, not overwhelmed by the opposition. He is sad that they 'do not believe' but is giving them another chance to understand.

Consider how certain the first-century Jews were that they knew what their Messiah would be and do. They had a simple way of thinking about him, simple and absolute. It was not to be challenged or tinkered with. Though the concept and hope was ancient, and centred on the realization of the Covenant, by the time of Jesus the Messiah was going to save the nation from the oppression of Rome.

Consider the muddled meanings we place upon the word today. It carries several associations and many hopes, be it 'priest', 'anointed one', or 'servant king'. Is he a national, political hero, or a redemptive personal saviour? What do we want Jesus to be? What did Jesus believe himself to be? When asked if he's the Christ, he describes himself as a shepherd. Remember, King David was a shepherd before he was a king. Jesus was not rejecting the traditional ideal of Messiah, but, as in all his handling of Jewish Scripture and beliefs, he was altering and developing the meaning, stretching it further and challenging the Jews to try out this new thought. Jesus would not have us limit the fullness of God's Covenant with us.

Pay attention in this passage to the number of times Jesus points away from himself to his Father, and pleads with his opponents to see that all he does, he does to glorify God.

Contemplate how Jesus and the Father can be one. Still your mind and contemplate how Jesus shares the same nature and essence as the Father. Contemplate how the whole of St John's Gospel, from the very beginning, stresses again and again that Jesus is the face of God. 'We have seen his glory' (John 1.14).

Contemplate how this gives us the certainty that if we give our lives to Jesus and follow him, we are already in the Father's hands, and no one can snatch us away.

As you desire to imitate him

Holy Father, greater than all,
Deepen my understanding of your oneness with your Son.
If I put myself into his hands
I will never be snatched from yours,
But led to eternal life.
Amen.

The Fifth Sunday of Easter

---•◆•---

John 13.31–35

Gaze on the supper table. The meal is over, the table strewn with crumbs, the cups empty of wine, and the plates greasy. The feast is finished and the disciples are tired. They are all anxious after they have been warned of betrayal, and confused by Judas' rapid departure. Surely now is the time to go home?

But gaze on Jesus. He has so much still to tell them, and he is only just getting into his stride! In John's Gospel we find Jesus embarking on a speech that lasts for another five chapters. Listen to Jesus talk of the glory of the Father and the gift of the Spirit and the imperative of love that this holds for us all. For everything is summed up in two short verses: 'Love one another. As I have loved you, so you must love one another. By this everyone will know that you are my disciples, if you love one another' (vv. 34 and 35, adapted).

Consider what this new commandment is saying to you now, in your situation today. What changes should you make to your attitudes, habits and behaviour, so that you may grow in love for another? Who in your life do you find it difficult to love? Think about the tension and criticism which is so prevalent in our neighbourhoods today, as we struggle to learn to live with diversity. Consider how Jesus consorted with outsiders and welcomed the stranger. Consider how we too, should be open to the Sikh across the road, or the Polish family round the corner.

Consider the difference between spontaneous love and deliberate love. Jesus was not expecting a wave of uncritical delight to wash over us, and make us ecstatically pleased to be in everyone's company, equally at ease with every member of our workplace, and open to the pleasures of every member of our extended family. He did not expect us to never again feel the grit of irritation.

Such spontaneous love only occurs a few times in our lives – for our children, who can do no wrong; for our lovers (at first); for a few precious friends.

But most of our loving must be of the other kind – a willed love that is related to duty, but carried out gladly because we are God's servant as the other is God's child. Such love makes us aware that we are no longer the centre of our small universe, and we become determined to put the other first, to respond to their needs and take their hopes seriously. This is a hard and difficult love to express and requires all the gifts of the Holy Spirit to achieve. Consider what they are: patience, encourage-ment, mercy, service and giving chief among them. Consider what gifts you have, and what gifts do you need to pray for?

Contemplate the way Jesus loved his disciples as individuals – ambitious James and John, vacillating and cowardly Peter, ques-tioning Thomas. But he never gave up on them. Contemplate the strangers and beggars and lepers he greeted and treated; imagine their ugliness, their stench, yet Jesus cared for them. Contemplate the paradox of the Christian way, how it was that God the Father could be glorified by the crucifixion of the Son.

As you desire to imitate him

Glorious God, I am called to imitate the great love Jesus had
for his disciples,
A love that was only possible through his love for you.
Fill my heart with this love and strengthen my will
To love the difficult people in my life and those that I fear.
Help me share love in the wasted places of this world,
For I long to be known as your disciple.
Amen.

The Sixth Sunday of Easter

John 14.23–29

Gaze on John, frowning with concentration as Jesus continues to deliver his lengthy 'farewell'. He is straining to remember it all, and to understand how all the twists and turns build into the overarching vindication of God's purpose in Jesus. Listen with John as Jesus pours out his heart, going over and over his message, trying to express it in as many ways as possible so that each of us may catch the one phrase or explanation that speaks to us today.

Gaze on John, years later, an old man, his hair thin and his back bent, fingers stained with ink, writing down his memories. Gaze on his pen which he used as a weaver would a shuttle, to form a tapestry of words, with the Father and the Son as warp and weft.

Consider peace, and how the world's ways bring such a poor version of it: at worst, with armies and barriers that divide people from people, even tearing families apart and breeding hatreds for the next generation to fight about; at best, with treaties and alliances that only remain in force while all sides benefit.

Then consider the peace that Jesus means. Consider the timescales of his peace, for there are two. The first is in the here and now, and is the inner peace he grants us if we follow his word and know his love. This is the peace you experience when you are secure in your motives and, though still bound up in the mess and conflict of humanity, certain of your next steps.

66

The second peace is far in the future, a kingdom we may not see in our generation, but one in which the whole world will be reconciled. And God will ask us, how did we help to bring it about?

Let go of the false hopes for a complacent life of dull contentment. Jesus is not promising that we will never be disturbed or that peace means an end to controversy. He is not promising a life of bliss. For Jesus' peace is intimately bound up with righteousness, and that will always involve a struggle.

Contemplate the promise that if we keep his word and love him, God the Father and the Son will make their home in us. Contemplate what you need to do to make your heart and life ready for Jesus to move in. What rooms must you spring-clean? What room needs redecorating? What dirty linen must you wash clean? What feast will you prepare?

As you desire to imitate him

Dear Father, soothe the troubled places of your world
And bring us peace.
Send your Spirit to the world,
And build up peace,
Keeping the promise made by your Son,
The Prince of Peace.
Amen.

The Seventh Sunday of Easter

John 17.20–26

Gaze on the disciples, trudging down the hillside after the Ascension, overwhelmed by the shock of losing the presence of Jesus yet again. Will absence make the heart grow fonder, or will it be a case of 'out of sight, out of mind'? Some are looking back, longing for it to have been a mistake, hoping against hope that they'll see Jesus where they left him, emerging from the mist, following after them towards Jerusalem. Some have their heads bowed, and look down, despondently, but they are resigned to his departure. Some are impatient, even cross – 'Well, now what do we do?' hear them say. Peter and John on the other hand, have their heads high; they are resolutely facing the city, determined to carry out Jesus' promises. Even if they feel abandoned by him, they will not let him down, knowing it's their message that Jesus is counting on now (v. 20).

Consider why, at the Ascension, the disciples might have recalled the words of Jesus' prayer for all believers: 'I pray for those who will believe in me through their message' (v. 20), and 'Father, I want those you have given me to be with me where I am' (v. 24). This was said only a few weeks earlier, though it seemed a lifetime ago, so much had happened in between.

Now the penny drops, and they understand the full oneness of Jesus with the Father. And so the realization dawns that of necessity the Father and Son must be reunited, and they, the disciples, separated from their leader. As night follows day, Jesus must return to his full glory.

But consider the encouragement and hope that these remembered words would have given them. They need not feel bereft, because Jesus' prayer assured them that they were all incorporated in this oneness. So, in time, they too would come to be with Jesus 'where I am'. They were not abandoned after all.

Contemplate the glory of the ascended Jesus. It is not the glory of diamonds or gold, ermine or palaces. But this glory arises from unity, and is a glory of strength, and steadiness, and everlasting love that such unity makes possible. The whole makes up so much more than the sum of the two parts. Contemplate the assurance we are given that this prayer is 'for those who *will* believe' – Jesus' ascension overcomes the dimensions of space and time, and includes us today in this unity of witness.

As you desire to imitate him

Dear Lord and King of glory,
Make me one with all who believe in you,
That the love we share
Will shine out and convince the world
That you were sent by the Father,
With whom you now reign in splendid unity.
Amen.

Day of Pentecost

John 14.8–17 [25–27]

Gaze on a wood in a storm, the trees blown every which way by the invisible wind. Branches are stripped of their leaves and the weaker boughs are broken, and fall to the forest floor. Listen to the rage of the storm, rushing through a garden, uprooting plants, howling around a house, and creaking in the eaves, battering at the window, desperate to get in. Now the storm has turned into a tornado, a once-in-a-lifetime event, lifting cars and caravans into the air, dumping them in gardens and conservatories, slicing roofs off houses. Next day, the entire landscape is changed.

Consider how this piece starts with the promise which John's Gospel begins with – if we want to know the Father, we must look at the Son. But now it goes further. Here is the Father in the Son, and the Son in the Father, and finally the Spirit of truth. It is almost as mysterious and complex as a mathematical proof scrawled out on the blackboard by a brilliant professor. And the outcome of all these equations is the ability to do great things (v. 12).

Or maybe this is the argument of a great barrister. For the word 'Counsellor' is not used in the modern sense of someone who listens in order to help us, but draws parallels with the legal profession where a counsel for the defence stands by you however much you are threatened. And a court of law should always be concerned with the truth, and the proof of innocence.

70

Finally, consider this as a chemical formula. For if we add all these ingredients together, the outcome will be a tremendous explosion of energy, and in the process we ourselves are re-created.

Contemplate the surprise that the disciples experienced when, with a rush of violent wind and tongues of fire, the Spirit of truth came to abide in them.

Contemplate how open you are to being surprised; how willing you are to be bowled over by God's power.

Contemplate letting the Spirit knock you sideways and turn you around, and send you out in a different direction entirely. Which way are you facing now?

As you desire to imitate him

Come, Holy Spirit,
Come as a gust of power,
Roll back the thunder clouds of sin
    And breathe into our world the spirit of peace.
Come as a breath of fresh air to our families;
Blow open closed doors,
    That the many who wait outside may enter in.
Come as a gentle summer's balm,
    To comfort the sick and distressed.
Come, Holy Spirit, come.
Amen.

ORDINARY TIME

Trinity Sunday

----◆----

John 16.12–15

Gaze on one of the great triptychs of medieval painting. These three-panelled paintings can be seen in all the great museums and some of the old cathedrals in Europe, displayed behind the altar. The main panel is flanked on either side by another, tilted slightly towards the centre, as if in conversation, but all three face out towards the congregation. Each is telling their own part of the story, but each is independent in its own right, and can be enjoyed on its own. By opening and shutting the panels, the observer can see different scenes, and take in different ideas: pictures of creation, sacrifice and inspiration, each important at different stages of our life, and each instructing us in something unique. Individual scenes can be a separate focus of prayer and devotion, and provide a journey of faith. But the whole is a unity, which is greater than all its parts. Over the centuries, some of these triptychs have become separated, but there is great excitement when they are reunited, and the full glory of the work is revealed.

Consider, at last, we have come to the end of our post-Easter time with John, delving into the farewell discourses, and unravelling the many meanings layered within. And now, in this passage, John is striving again to explain the intensely close connection between the Spirit of truth and Jesus – 'He will bring glory to me by taking from what is mine and making it known to you' (v. 14) – but not in any competitive way, and not in a way that will diminish or weaken Jesus. And if that is not complicated enough, Jesus then tells us that this 'mine' which he has shared with the Spirit is also of the Father. All of this is a giving away; none of it is a hanging on to power, for there is no possessiveness in the nature of the Trinity at all. Has not Jesus told us again and again that to give is to gain? Consider when relationships are really fruitful, how they produce of themselves much to share with others. Like the triptychs, they face outwards to others.

Consider the relationships in your life – are they strong enough to avoid possessiveness? Are they rich enough to share with others? Consider what you need to do to strengthen your relationships, in order to build them into models of the Trinity.

Contemplate this description of 'wisdom's call' from today's Old Testament Lesson (Proverbs 8.22–32). 'The Lord brought me forth as the first of his works . . . I was appointed from eternity . . . before the world began . . . Then I was the craftsman at his side. I was filled with delight day after day . . . and delighting in mankind.'

As you desire to imitate him

Gracious Father, bless all my relationships.
Loving Jesus, teach me to put the other first.
Spirit of wisdom, strengthen my understanding,
So that I may build and not destroy.
Holy Trinity, turn the bonds of my relationships into loving
    links
Not prison chains, and let me delight daily in the love of
    others.
Amen.

Proper 4

———◆———

Luke 7.1–10

Gaze on the expression of amazement on Jesus' face. He is overjoyed by this man's witness of faith and his willingness to submit to the spiritual authority of a local itinerant teacher of a subjugated nation. Think how encouraged he must have been by the behaviour of this centurion, a foreigner, yet deferring to him, a member of the subjugated people.

Gaze on the centurion when he realizes his servant has been healed. Does he accept the cure as nothing less than he expected, or is he astonished, despite his earlier protestations of faith? We are not told if he even meets Jesus, for it is the intermediaries who return to the house and find the servant healed.

Gaze on the crowds, and hear their exclamations of delight and surprise. Do they hear the subtle rebuke in Jesus' words (v. 9)?

Consider how this story follows so well from the passage immediately above it in Luke, which concludes the Sermon on the Plain (which mirrors Matthew's Sermon on the Mount). In that, Jesus has told us to love our enemies and be careful not to judge others, and he's told us how the good man brings good out of the store of his heart. Now here we have a gentile, a Roman centurion, who is a good man and caring master and even a benefactor to the local synagogue. The good man can come from any nation, tribe or culture. He could have been seen as an enemy, but is admired by his Jewish neighbours. Here we have a rare glimpse in the Gospels of a neighbourhood living in harmony, one that follows the precepts of Jesus' great sermon. Here is an example of the power that following the way of Jesus will produce. Here is a picture of what is possible in small countries where people with different backgrounds and competing power bases love and respect each other, without pre-judging (from which we get the word prejudice, of course).

Consider the words of the centurion: 'But say the word, and my servant will be healed.' If you are a regular attender at an Anglican Eucharist, these words will be familiar. We, like the centurion, will never meet Jesus face to face on this earth. But in the Eucharist, we can approach Jesus and know that he will listen to us.

Contemplate what this story tells us about the manner in which we should offer our petitions to Jesus. We should be *bold* and dare to believe that Jesus is there to help us; we should be *brave* and seize the opportunity; we should acknowledge the authority of Jesus, granted him by his Father, and therefore be *humble*, knowing it is not our worthiness but Jesus' all-encompassing love that means we will be heard.

As you desire to imitate him

Dear Jesus, Grant me faith in your power and hear my earnest
    plea.
I bring before you all the people known to me who are in
    need today,
Especially [. . . *here include your own intercessions* . . .].
Say the word, and heal all those for whom I pray.
Amen.

Proper 5

---◆◆◆---

Luke 7.11–17

Gaze on a funeral scene in Britain – everyone is in their best clothes, dark, sombre and formal. People make an effort to contain their emotions and no one wants to 'break down' in public. We put on a brave face and give thanks for the life lost. If it is a young person who is being buried, it is much harder, for the emotions are more raw, the confusion and pain so much nearer the surface, and the sobbing is louder, but still we cling to our dignity, our true feelings locked away in the closed coffin.

Gaze on a funeral anywhere in the Middle East. We have seen too many on the TV news lately, but they haven't changed much since Jesus' time. There is no attempt to hide the grief, the people keen and the women ululate, as their bodies bend double and they beat their chests. And the body on the bier is openly displayed, held high above the crowds, as was the widow's son in Nain.

Consider how this story forms a pair with last week's when Jesus helped a powerful man who was a gentile. Now he helps a defenceless widow. But both of them, in their way, were outsiders. Consider how the crowd reacts to this miracle: they exclaim, 'God has come to help his people'. In this way they expand a single miracle of a life restored to signify much more. They see it as a sign of God's desire to save and redeem in many ways more than the curing of one individual, for how could that actually 'help his people'?

Consider what help these people really needed – health, yes, but freedom too. They needed restoration of liberty and dignity in a country oppressed by a foreign empire and corrupt local rulers.

Consider what help our nation needs from God today. Yes, we would love to banish all pain and suffering, and the tragic death of the young to be prevented. But what are the real sufferings of our people? Are they not fear of the stranger, mistrust of our leaders, and worry over the rapidity of change which leaves us insecure? Are they not fear for the future of our children and our planet in a time of climate change, where present greed smothers the sacrifices we know we should make to sustain the future? Are they not fear of isolation, of futility, and of extinction?

Consider where the help to cure all this dis-ease can come from.

Contemplate how personal Jesus' reaction was: 'his heart went out to her and he said, "Don't cry"', just as we do to someone who is grieving and distressed. When we say, 'Don't cry' it is often a helpless, useless exclamation, an instant reaction to try in vain to ease the pain. But Jesus' distress was not in vain and his touch was full of power and he raised the son to new life.

Contemplate Jesus' heart going out to you today: what worry or pain do you want him to heal?

As you desire to imitate him

Dear Jesus when I grieve, please touch me;
When others grieve, may I touch them.
When I cry, please comfort me;
When others cry, may I comfort them.
May my heart be open to the needs of others,
And when I die may you be there
To raise me to new life.
Amen.

Proper 6

———◆◆◆———

Luke 7.36—8.3

Gaze at the dinner party and all the guests reclining on couches, facing the table, their legs stretched out behind them. This is how it is that the woman can stand behind Jesus at his feet, bathe them with her tears, dry them with her hair, and smother them with perfume.

Smell the food cooking and the smoke from the roasting meat turning on the spit. Taste the succulent lamb, scattered with herbs; dip bread into the oil. Hear the bustle of the servants and the satisfaction of the guests, smacking their lips with gusto. Share with the woman the feeling of being blessed when Jesus turns to her, not in irritation but with gladness.

Consider what this story tells us about the position of women in that time. Women knew their place, and 'fallen' women knew it more than anyone. There was a hierarchy even among sinners. The woman here dared only stand behind Jesus. Simon the Pharisee must have been outraged at her interrupting his dinner party. And this woman, like the woman who crept up to touch Jesus' cloak, expects rejection, and is used to being shunned. She doesn't have the confidence even to speak – her actions must speak for her.

Consider why this gospel passage goes on to tell us about other women, those who went with the twelve. Luke is determined for us to know that Jesus treated women with equality and gave them the right to participate. Their names are remembered today, but there are still societies in the world where women are excluded and their dignity denied. Consider how, for once, Jesus is dining with the in-crowd, a well-to-do member of the hierarchy. For once he's not consorting with tax collectors or prostitutes. Yet even here a well-known sinner seeks him out and shames the Pharisee by her humility. For Simon the Pharisee is thrice rebuked – '*You did not . . .*' Jesus tells him, comparing his meanness with the man in the story who only owed a little. How well Jesus knew human nature.

Contemplate which character you are in this story. Do you behave and think like Simon – small-minded, self-righteous and unbending, but basically missing the point? Or are you this woman, aware of your sins and begging for a new beginning?

As you desire to imitate him

Dear God, I acknowledge my great debt to you.
I am a sinner, in need of your forgiveness.
I confess all the times I have not cared for you,
Through lack of care of others.
I give you thanks that you have cancelled what I owe,
And pledge myself to repay you with love.
Amen.

Proper 7

———•◆•———

Luke 8.26–39

Gaze on all that is unclean in this story: the man himself, the tombs he lived in, and the pigs feeding on swill, caked with mud. Gaze on the vagrants of our cities today: the men stretched out on newspaper in the shop doorways; bag ladies pushing trolleys full of jumble and rubbish; young men with long grubby hair and flea-ridden dogs; all in bad need of a bath.

They have no home to go to, and live in the tombs of our cities – gutters, underpasses, archways, and hidden on building sites. Gaze on the drunks, whose lives have been ruined by 'the demon drink'. Gaze on the many homeless who are mentally ill and who have no one to care for them and ensure they take their medication. Gaze on their odd behaviour which makes us uneasy and their dirtiness which makes us queasy. It is so much easier just to look away.

Consider the fate of people with mental illness in pre-scientific ages. They were condemned to be treated as possessed by demons, and cast out from society to live in tombs – as if they were already dead to society. How slowly our attitudes to mental illness have changed! Consider how comfortable you feel still when you are near someone whose behaviour goes beyond the norms of the socially acceptable. Ask yourself how ready you would have been to approach someone like this, let alone ask him or her 'What is your name?' Perhaps it was the closeness that Jesus displayed by asking his name which was the beginning of his healing.

Consider why the bystanders who saw this miracle should be in the grip of a great fear. Consider how you would feel if you witnessed such an event. We assume they should be happy for the person, yet this is not their first reaction. What were they so afraid of? In some ways perhaps it is right to be afraid of such power. But why beg Jesus to go, when he has just done such good?

Consider next how Jesus commissions the man as an evangelist: 'Return home and tell how much God has done for you.' So this down-and-out returns, someone who was once the lowest of the low. And Jesus expects him to be received as a messenger of good news. Consider how likely – or unlikely – it was, that the self-satisfied would listen to one such as him.

Consider how easy you find it to tell others how much God has done for you. Do you remember to acknowledge his power in your life?

Contemplate Jesus' question to the devils: 'What is your name?' Which evils have you come across in your life? What torments do you cling on to? It is so important that we name the fears that plague us. Once they are named, they are so much less frightening; for once shaped, they are no longer limitless.

Bring one, by name, to Jesus now. Ask him to drive it from you.

As you desire to imitate him

Most High God, I long to be made clean
And free of all that torments me,
My fears and my sins which stop me living
In your abundance.
I give thanks that you so willingly release me,
And pledge myself to tell of your power in my life.
Amen.

Proper 8

———•◦•———

Luke 9.51–62

Gaze on the sort of journeys we make today, on all the preparation and paraphernalia we acquire. We need tickets and passports, hotel reservations, luggage and currency. We surround ourselves with so much security, and so much comfort, and find it hard to travel light. How we moan about the restrictions on the weight of our luggage on the plane! Gaze on Jesus and his disciples: reliant on the hospitality of strangers, sleeping out in the open if necessary, determined not to rely on anything that will handicap their swiftness and entice them to stay any longer than they need. They do not relax by the pool, or linger over a three-course lunch. They are always concerned to travel on, looking ahead to the next stop, for their message is urgent and there are always more people ahead who need to hear it.

Consider how harsh Jesus sounds in this piece – 'Let the dead bury their own dead.' Yet we know how compassionate he was about the death of loved ones, for we see him caring for the bereaved and restoring the dead to life. So it cannot be that he is being disrespectful here, or unfeeling. So what is it he really means?

We see two opposing attitudes – one a man rashly blurting out 'I'll follow you', only to be warned to think carefully before committing himself. On the other hand, another whom Jesus calls appears to do just that – he must bury his father (a duty that all Jews would acknowledge) – only to be told by Jesus to get on with proclaiming the Kingdom. A sense of urgency is beginning to dominate Jesus' message and ministry.

Consider how Jesus is using this message to challenge us. Do we want to be left behind as if dead ourselves, no longer able to respond to his call, and no longer willing to work in his service? Or are we prepared to live life today to its full, to follow him wherever he goes and face the risks this will entail?

We are being asked to consider if we are spiritually dead, or spiritually alive.

Contemplate why Jesus warns us not to look back. For sometimes we look back with nostalgia, and that is self-indulgent. Sometimes we look back with sorrow, which can become self-pity. Sometimes we look back in anger, which can turn to bitterness. And sometimes we look back with shame, which can turn to despair. If we look back to learn, ready to let go of the good and repent of the bad, then Jesus will walk into the future with us.

As you desire to imitate him

Lord of the journey, release me from false attachments to this
    world;
Free me from the places and habits I cling to.
Make me ready to put my hand
To whatever service you ask of me,
And to follow you even to persecution
Just as you strode on to Jerusalem.
Amen.

Proper 9

Luke 10.1–11, 16–20

Gaze on yourself as you arrive in a town for the first time. Have you booked your hotel room ahead, or are you leaving it to chance? Recall the strange street signs, the one-way system that confuses and traps you, and the difficulty in finding a place to park. Which is the way to the cathedral – left or right, and where is a good place for dinner?

Now gaze on the 72, scattered across the country in pairs and wandering into towns they've never been to before. In small villages they stick out like sore thumbs; they can't be inconspicuous and anonymous like a modern traveller. Here, the arrival of a stranger is a big event. All eyes are on them, and they hold their breath, unsure whether they will be received with friendship or hostility.

How often we return from a holiday and comment, 'The locals were quite friendly' – how important that is to us! Imagine how much more it must have been for the 72. Jesus made no bones about how difficult it would be – lambs among wolves indeed! We'd never dream of going somewhere that had that in the guidebook.

Consider the good news tucked away in this passage, which otherwise is rather stern and alarming. It is this: Jesus doesn't expect us to go out alone. Even if we are like lambs among wolves, Jesus sends us out two by two, for he always gives us the support we need. We do not have to think it is all down to us.

We can and must share the task with others, for we all have different strengths and weaknesses.

Consider how much easier it is to find your way if you have another person with you to study the map. Consider how much less frightening problems are when you have someone else to talk them through with; how much easier it is to laugh. Consider how much courage it gives you to be with another – courage enough to ask questions, or make a fool of yourself, even. Consider who you might go out with to do God's work.

Consider how often we weigh up beforehand whether our overture will be accepted or rejected, and if we guess we'll be rejected, we just don't try. But that is not allowed by Jesus. We are expected to go into the streets and really make ourselves noticed.

Contemplate our countryside in late summer. Farmers worry over the weather and dread the rain that batters the crops and prevents them reaping the wheat. For there is only a certain time when the harvest can be collected – too early, and the crop will not be ripe, and it will be worthless; too late and it will be damaged, stale and useless.

Contemplate what Jesus is saying to you through this. Where are you called to act today?

Contemplate what happens when such moments are missed.

As you desire to imitate him

Lord of the harvest, make me brave enough
To work in your fields,
Even as a lamb among wolves.
Give me a companion to encourage me,
And trust that with your Spirit as partner,
We will bring in the Kingdom.
Amen.

Proper 10

—•◦•—

Luke 10.25–37

Gaze on the victim in this story, the traveller who has been mugged and beaten and left in a stinking alleyway, bleeding and sore, miles from home. Imagine you are that victim. Someone comes near and hears your moans. He peers down at you.

But look! He is a young man in a hood, with rings in his nose, eyebrows and lips, his arms are tattooed, his jeans are torn – just the sort of person whom you least trust!

Or, look! He is a Muslim with a dark beard and looks just like a terrorist on the front page of the newspaper.

But look! He is a Palestinian from Gaza and you are an Orthodox Jewish settler living on land he claims as his. You shrink further away from him for fear of another beating.

Consider the importance of this story, for it is quite devalued if it is just used to teach us to be kind to our neighbours. Jesus tells it as the answer to the question, 'What must I do to inherit eternal life?' It is as important as that. And another crucial point is how, in this parable, Jesus is extending the definition of neighbour far beyond the limits accepted in the Old Testament. For these two men had never met before.

This story is about love of a stranger who was deliberately accepted as a neighbour, but Jesus starts by referring to the law, to a law that we must obey (v. 26). Though Jesus sat lightly to many rules and regulations of his day, this is not a law he is prepared to overturn or trivialize, or for us to ignore when it suits us. This law is God's law and it must be obeyed if we are to live

(v. 28). For the newness of this teaching was that the law was love. In this way Jesus turned what had been negative into a positive, and a burden into a release. The parable shows us that fear of others can be banished by reaching out to them. It is these changes to how we live our lives today that will bring us into his eternal presence.

Contemplate your prejudices – the groups of people whom you shun and criticize and dismiss. Name them and bring them into Jesus' presence. Contemplate loving them, and the consequences this will have for your life.

As you desire to imitate him

Neighbour Jesus, teach me to recognize the image of God in
    all people;
Help me to root out my prejudices and irrational fears of
    others;
Guide me into love of all strangers whom I meet.
May I greet them with mercy
And together with them inherit eternal life.
Amen.

Proper 11

———◆———

Luke 10.38–42

Gaze at Martha, inviting Jesus in for a rest and a meal. How she wants to please him! She is bustling about humming quietly to herself with pleasure. She dashes round with the duster, then sets the cushions straight. Next she potters in the kitchen, getting the food ready, chopping and boiling and stirring. But she is beginning to get a bit hot and bothered now. Her hair is escaping her scarf. Time seems to be rushing along and she is nowhere near ready. Her early good humour is beginning to turn sour. She can smell something burning on the stove, and still the table needs laying. Surely Mary can do that? Feel her rising anger. Do you share it? Taste her resentment and her frustration that once again she, Martha, is relegated to the kitchen, unnoticed and overlooked.

Gaze on the lives of the many women in the poor countries of this world who are still burdened by chores. They must spend hours searching for firewood, then walk two, three or more miles to fetch water, before they can make the bread to feed their family.

Consider how this story contrasts with the one we read last week about the Good Samaritan. Surely he was another 'Martha' – someone willing to help. So what makes Jesus' response so different? We know that Jesus himself took care to meet the practical needs of the crowds when they were hungry, making sure they were provided for. So surely he would approve of

Martha's efforts? Consider why he seems to be contradicting himself now, by telling Martha to stop.

Look at where this story comes in Luke's Gospel, and then consider how it fits in with earlier warnings Jesus has given. The disciples were warned not to hang about in towns and villages if their message was rejected, for the harvest was too important. And just before that, Luke has reported an even more urgent message, when Jesus says, 'Let the dead bury their own dead.' Now consider Martha's behaviour in conjunction with these stories. It begins to make sense, for Jesus is warning her not to miss the present moment and opportunity.

Contemplate Jesus' response to Martha: 'You are worried and upset about many things' (v. 41). Contemplate how this rushing around of Martha's differs from the caring of the Good Samaritan. Contemplate how easy it is to avoid the important moments by concentrating on the seemingly urgent.

Contemplate what it is in your life that distracts you most often from 'the better way'.

As you desire to imitate him

Dear Jesus, bless those whose lives are full
Of daily drudgery, and who toil to care for their families.
Enable them to find time
For praise and contemplation.
May I keep in proportion my daily tasks,
And always find time to devote to you.
Amen.

Proper 12

—•◆•—

Luke 11.1–13

Gaze on a clear night sky, full of stars, and a partial moon that lights up your way along the narrow village streets. Hear the frantic banging, waking everyone in the house. Who can it be at this time of night – there must be a fire somewhere, or a death. But it is only your friend, knocking at your midnight door. Hear him begging you to open up and lend him the bread he needs to feed his guest, so that he is not humiliated as host. At first you don't want to be bothered. But his persistence wins you over. At least if you give in you'll get back to bed.

Imagine the boldness of the man making the request, and his sense of desperation. Hear the bolts as you draw them back, and the door opening, at first just a crack, and then wide enough for the gift to be given. See the look of relief on his face.

Consider how this passage follows the story of Mary sitting at the feet of the Lord. And now Jesus is teaching us what we should be saying when we are sitting at his feet. Jesus is not adding to the shelves of self-help manuals in today's bookshops that tell us how to centre ourselves and still ourselves and create the space and mood to pray. He is not telling us to light a candle or choose an icon or repeat a mantra; although elsewhere, by example, he shows us how important it is at times to withdraw and choose a quiet place.

Rather, this prayer is a statement of Jesus' creed. First and foremost it is about *relationships*: with the Father and Creator, and between ourselves and God. It is about the *conditions* we must fulfil for our prayers to be acceptable, chiefly right relationship with our neighbour (when we pray for forgiveness); and it is about the kind of *outcomes* and hopes we are entitled to pray for: the coming of the Kingdom here on earth, and the good gifts of the Holy Spirit (v. 13).

Consider how the rest of this passage develops the idea of relationship. We are told about a friend in need, and a parent responding to their child's requests. Consider how this reinforces the first line of the prayer: Abba, Father.

Contemplate the care with which you choose presents for those you love best in the world. If you have ever had children, remember the delight you took in their faces when they opened their birthday present, or explored their Christmas stocking.

Contemplate the joy you felt when they showed you'd chosen just the right thing, and when you heard them say, 'It's perfect.'

Contemplate our God and Father, who knows these tender emotions and shares this urge to shower us with good gifts.

As you desire to imitate him

Listening and Holy Lord, teach me to pray.
Help me be in right relationship with my neighbour and sister
    and brother,
So that I have the right to accept the good gifts of the Holy
    Spirit,
Which by your love you are longing to give me.
Amen.

Proper 13

————◆◆◆————

Luke 12.13–21

Gaze on an allotment in high summer. All the fruits and vegetables are ripening together, for the profligacy of nature takes us by surprise every time. Every year we grow more beans than we can hope to use. There's a bumper crop of gooseberries, and the raspberries go on and on, and now the plums are falling off the tree. Tomatoes are turned into chutney and apples are for pudding every day, even after you've taken bags into the office, or left them at the back of the church.

Gaze on your freezer, full to the brim. Is this not the modern equivalent of this man's barn? And come next year, there will be old bags lurking at the bottom, labels missing, for it is impossible to use up all the largesse of the harvest.

Consider what we were taught last week in the Lord's Prayer, and remember the illustrations Jesus chose – a neighbour sharing bread, and a father feeding his son. And now a man comes up to Jesus and asks that his brother share his inheritance with him. Surely that is exactly what Jesus will approve of? Yet Jesus disagrees and his reply goes far beyond the obvious. He tells the man his envy is as unloving as his brother's unwillingness to share. For both show that their greatest desire is for material wealth.

Consider what this tells us about recent turmoil in our banking industry. We have put our faith in something that did not deserve our trust, and has shown itself to be of false value.

Consider how alarming it has been. Many have feared they might lose their savings. Stocks and shares are the barns of our society, and banks the storehouses where we lay up good things for the future. But they have proved unsafe, and we are exposed as greedy as the rich fool. As Christians, what does this tell us about how tethered we still are to this world?

Consider how Jesus ends this story. The criticism of the farmer's greed for hoarding in the barns is implicit. But Jesus is warning of something even more important. For we must remember we do not ultimately control our lives. So what good will possessions be when the rich man dies? The farmer and the man in the crowd both fell into the same trap, worse than greed. They thought they were in charge of their own destiny.

Contemplate what riches you have to share. Contemplate what talents you have to put to the service of others. How often do you use them for the greater good, and how often do you take life easy and enjoy them for yourself? Contemplate your current charitable giving, and whether it is equal to Jesus' expectations.

As you desire to imitate him

Dear Lord, your world is abundant with produce and riches
    enough for all.
I thank you for the harvest and pray for ways to share it with
    others.
May I never assume your bounty belongs to me,
For my hands were empty at my birth
And will be empty once more at my death.
Amen.

Proper 14

———•◆•———

Luke 12.32–40

Gaze on the vault of a bank, excavated deep below street level. It has triple walls made of steel and iron, and the doors are bolted and double locked. Only a few people know the combination of the safe inside. Stacked there, from floor to ceiling, are flimsy pieces of paper with vague pictures of the famous, and strange writing. How would a stranger from outer space ever guess they were so valuable that they needed this level of protection?

Gaze on the Securicor guards, helmeted and wearing heavy jackets and big boots. Their van windows barred. Bags of coins are piled up inside.

Gaze on your Bible. No one will try to steal that. No need to keep that in a safe place.

Consider why Jesus continues on immediately from saying, 'Where your treasure is, there your heart will be also', to the words, 'Be dressed ready for service'. Consider what connects these two ideas, for on the face of it they do not automatically follow on. But consider more carefully: if your heart is fixed on a heavenly kingdom it will not be weighed down by worldly care. You will be light of foot and speedy in responding to God's will.

Jesus is continuing the lesson we learnt last week, not to store up our savings or hoard nature's excess in barns or safes, but to live from day to day. But now he is taking it on a stage further to show us the damage we suffer if we keep hold of our possessions. He is saying it is not just morally wrong to be so greedy, but that greed will turn us from the priorities of our lives, and stop us being keen and active in his cause.

Finally, Jesus is yet again injecting a sense of urgency into our lives, the same urgency he's underlined in previous readings.

Contemplate your daily priorities and your weekly routine. Contemplate how you like best to spend your time and money. Contemplate where most of your energy goes. For where you place your energy will show you what you treasure most – the result may surprise you.

Another way of saying this is, what are the values that govern how you live?

As you desire to imitate him

Dear Jesus, may I be alert when you come,
Dressed and ready for action.
Help me let go of temporary delights
And place my trust in the gift of your word.
Then, by your good pleasure,
My heart will be open to receive the Kingdom.
Amen.

Proper 15

———•◆•———

Luke 12.49–56

Gaze on the sky as yet another weather front approaches. Dirty clouds lurk overhead, and the rain begins to lash down at some unseen trigger. How the weather can affect our moods! We are so much more content and kind when the sky is blue. Gaze on the TV evening weather forecast. There is the picture of Britain, with all the symbols sweeping over it. Yellow suns are brightening the west; the north is plunged into grey again. Or vice versa. We listen intently and 'take it as gospel'. Until it turns out wrong – then listen to us moan and criticize the forecasters! For in Britain, our weather is far from predictable. Perhaps Jesus would not have chosen his examples of clouds bringing rain, and wind bringing heat, had he lived here. Yet even we have country lore and sayings that predict the weather.

Consider how for the past two weeks we have been hearing of the dangers of hanging on to wealth. If you aren't 'rich', you may consider that Jesus isn't meaning you. But other precious belongings can cut us off from Jesus, too. If we were asked what was dearer to us than money, most of us would say our family. Consider how families may differ in so many ways, but all except for the absolute failures provide us with the security and love which we cannot live without. Consider again what Jesus is saying – even this you may have to give up for his sake. Now that really would be a sacrifice.

Consider how hard this message is. But sometimes it is true that love of one's family can become so insular that it is an excuse for not responding to the needs of others around you. So we must make sure we don't use our family as an excuse for ignoring the Kingdom. How often we interpret the old saying 'Charity begins at home' as meaning 'Charity should stay at home'.

And consider when Jesus is saying this. He is beginning to understand more clearly the threat he is living under and the danger he is moving towards. He is anticipating a world turned upside down where chaos in relationships will be one of the symptoms of change. In this mood, Jesus sees all the anguish and anger of the human condition. He has absorbed it and is reflecting it back to his listeners. These were the signs of the end of time; this was the world picture that Jesus grew up with. So we need not interpret this warning as saying that family divisions must be our norm. Quite the opposite, for Jesus took this as a sign that the present age was coming to an end.

Contemplate how we should interpret the present time. Do we read our newspaper prayerfully? Where are the storm clouds gathering today? Surely over Israel and Palestine again. Where is there fire and division? In Iraq, the Congo, Darfur and Afghanistan. Where is there chaos? In our financial markets.

All areas of life are beset by division, maybe even close to home, in your workplace or your city or your family. But if you read the very next paragraph (vv. 57–59), Jesus tells us how to heal these divisions – 'Try hard to be reconciled' (with your adversary).

Contemplate today who you should try to be reconciled with; then do something about it.

As you desire to imitate him

Dear Jesus, guide me through all the dangers of this present age.
Give me insight to interpret the signs,
So that I can act wisely and respond quickly
When you call on me to mend this troubled world.
Amen.

Proper 16

Luke 13.10–17

Gaze on the woman, bent double from her youth. Slowly her shoulders curved. Left behind by sisters who married, she remained alone, ridiculed, and treated as an outcast. Children shouted 'Hunchback!' at her. She made friends with ants and caterpillars and marvelled at the anemones in the spring. Her only chance to gaze at the moon was in a rare puddle of rain. She saw the high Judaean hills only as reflections in the lake. But she has waited and listened and learnt the wisdom of patience, and the patience of the wise. She saw only a fragment of life. But who really sees the whole?

Consider the marvel of this story. It seems that the woman does not beg or pray for a cure. She does not creep up and touch him, as another suffering woman once did. She does not rely on friends to lower her through the roof to Jesus' feet, or on family to hasten out on the road to gain Jesus' attention. No, this woman is in the synagogue expecting nothing. But 'Jesus saw her'.

Consider how all-seeing Jesus is. He sees us in our need. He sees us in our sins – and then we are less comfortable, for we would rather hide from him at such times. When we act in ways less than loving, when our words betray us or our heart is hard, we act as if God isn't looking, but we fool ourselves.

Consider how Jesus uses this healing as an example of the priority of releasing people from the shackles which bind – some imposed from society, others we chose ourselves. Jesus expected his critics to realize this healing was an explanation of the people's plight. For he was offering to set the rulers free from the yoke that bound them and the people to petty rules that burdened without any benefit.

Consider how one of Jesus' most scathing criticisms was to call someone 'hypocrite'. A hypocrite knows the truth but prefers to dissemble, feels one thing but acts differently, isn't ignorant, but prefers the expedient to the truth. A hypocrite is divided within himself, but an honest person is at peace.

Contemplate someone you know who is bent double. They may be bent double by pain or grief, or by guilt. Contemplate how crippling guilt is. How it gnaws away like a cancer, and spreads its poison through the system.

Place that person in front of Jesus where he can see her or him. He will not ignore their suffering. What part does Jesus want you to play in helping them stand straight again?

As you desire to imitate him

Dear Jesus, I am bound by sin
And stiffened by guilt.
I bind others with unnecessary expectations –
Release them from my judgement,
And open my eyes to my hypocrisy.
Lord Jesus, straighten me, and set me free
To glorify you for ever.
Amen.

Proper 17

─◆─

Luke 14.1, 7–14

Gaze on a very common social situation – everyone arrives at a 'do', and there are several round tables laid up with glittering candles and vases of freesia and crisp white napkins. People are hovering about, for none wants to be the first to be seated, in case no one chooses to sit next to them. But neither do they want to leave it too late to choose a place, in case they get stuck next to the bore. Minds are making swift calculations as to who it will be worthwhile sitting near. Who looks most important, most interesting, or most handsome? Who might be the most useful business connection?

Gaze on the alternative situation, where the host has placed everyone in advance. You search for your name card, and finally find, to your embarrassment, that you are trapped next to the person invited to make up the numbers. Everyone knows he or she is a person of no significance, and by being seated with them, are you belittled too?

Consider how many times Jesus has made this point. How many times has he repeated this message: 'Everyone who exalts himself will be humbled, and he who humbles himself will be exalted' (v. 11). In other words, the first must be last, and you must be the servant. Jesus hammers home this message in parable after parable, and more clearly in his teachings and actions with his disciples. It is in capital letters in the Beatitudes. Try counting how often he tells us this. It is probably more often than he actually tells us to *love*.

Consider, what is loving another, if it is not putting them first? Love doesn't often remain that first intense emotion of 'falling in love'. And there are other people in the world to love, not only your partner. Love must be transformed by the will into a pattern of behaviour which considers the well-being of another before your own. So all Jesus' teaching about putting others first is describing the activities which constitute a loving relationship. Far better to give us concrete examples of what love looks like in action than vague exhortations 'to love'.

Consider the other very important point this passage makes about love, without actually using the word. It is that we give to those we love without expectation of receiving anything in return. We love without demanding we are paid. We love freely and without terms and conditions.

Contemplate the meaning of real Christian hospitality. If you were to throw the sort of party Jesus describes here, who would you invite?

Contemplate how many of the social groupings you belong to you joined for love's sake and how many because you might gain some advantage in return.

Contemplate how often, even unconsciously, we divide people up between those to bother with or not. Contemplate how careful we should be – which of these groups would Jesus say we belong to?

As you desire to imitate him

Dear Jesus, may I make friends with the poor
And sit next to the rejected.
May I welcome the ignored
And invite the undeserving into my home.
May I practise true Christian hospitality
And express your love to all I meet.
Amen.

Proper 18

————◆•◆————

Luke 14.25–33

Gaze on a woman baking a fruit cake for a celebration. The ingredients take up half a page in the recipe book. She checks them off one by one – butter, sugar, flour, raisins, sultanas, cherries . . . Smell the fruit, and the pungent spices! But she has no eggs. Without them, what will bind the cake together? She will bake a stodgy mess, fit only as crumbs for the birds. The cake baking must wait until she's been to the shops.

Gaze on a tailor, cutting out the material for a made-to-measure suit. Feel the softness of the material; see its bright sheen, and the criss-cross of chalk marks. But he has under-estimated the length of cloth he needs and ends up with the front and the back but only one sleeve. What a waste of effort. No one can wear a jacket with only one sleeve.

Not many of us want to build a tower or wage war against a king. But we can all imagine tasks in our lives that are the equivalent.

Consider how Jesus is leading us deeper and deeper into the core of living the loving life. This holds true for living in love with others as much as it does for living for love of God. We learnt last week some of the 'cost' of loving – putting others first, and not expecting recompense. Love can be an asymmetrical relationship. For instance, the love of a parent for a child is almost always stronger and longer lasting than that of a child for the parent. But that does not stop the parent loving the child.

Consider how now we are being warned that before entering into the responsibility of relationships – before making our marriage vows, or before pledging ourselves at confirmation – we should be prepared to estimate the cost. Some foresight is expected of us, and the willingness to plan. Jesus doesn't want us to throw ourselves into change on a wave of emotion and expect that to carry us through. We must enter with our eyes open. And what a price it is we might be asked to pay! Once more Jesus takes the most outrageous example he can think of, one that we will be most reluctant to accept – our family. That is why he chooses it, to show us the enormity of what might be called for. For possessions are more than flash cars, luxury holidays, or diamond jewellery. The possessions Jesus refers to are anything that roots us to this world and fills our arms so that we have no room left in which to carry our cross.

Contemplate what in this life you have begun to build. Is it called 'My Desire' or is it dedicated to God? Is the builder A. Whim and Co., or is it The Kingdom and Son?

What do you need to be able to complete it?

As you desire to imitate him

Dear Lord, help me prepare by prayer
And practise by action
To give up my most precious possessions
In order to build your Kingdom.
Grant me the persistence to finish
What I have begun to build for your sake.
Amen.

Proper 19

———•◦•———

Luke 15.1–10

Gaze on the hunt for a set of lost keys. Your panic rises as you riffle through your handbag or pockets, searching for the door key. You're locked out and it's cold and wet. What can be worse than that?

Gaze on the hunt for a child lost in the supermarket. See the panic etched on the parents' faces as they race from aisle to aisle calling the child's name. Smell their fear, feel the sweat on their palms, hear their heartbeats thudding like a drum.

Hear the manager call over the tannoy, 'Would the parents of little Jo come to the information desk where your son is waiting for you.' Share the parents' surge of relief and watch them engulf the child in cuddles, smothering him with kisses. They are rejoicing in his return, swearing never to let him out of their sight again.

Consider how the Pharisees are hounding Jesus with more and more vigour, but the tax collectors and sinners who are gathered around him understand who the sheep and the coin really are. Consider how most of us in the West will react if we lose a £5 note. Is it any longer a cause for panic? Probably not, unless you are someone relying on state benefits and then you will immediately empathize with these descriptions.

Next, consider, really consider, what some people in this world suffer when they lose a coin, or a loaf of bread, or spill a bucket of water. For people who live on the very edge of poverty, that loaf is the difference between starvation and survival for their family that day. If a bucket of water is spilt, they know they must walk five miles to the well and five miles back to replenish it, or else the family could die of thirst or risk infections from dirty water. Try to understand this fear that the poor live with day by day. Then we might understand the full impact that this story would have had on the people to whom Jesus was preaching.

Contemplate God's free love of us: 'God demonstrates his own love for us in this: While we were still sinners, Christ died for us' (Romans 5.8). God's love is always ready and waiting, it is never lost to us, but we wander off and get separated from him by our own will and actions, like the wilful child in the supermarket. Then we no longer experience his love.

Contemplate the sin that you most regret, the one which today stands most in the way between you and the joy of the presence of God.

As you desire to imitate him

Dear Lord and Father, forgive my frequent falling short:
The right action avoided,
My careless neglect of other's needs,
The hurtful habit of thought.
May my repentance be true and lasting
So that you may welcome my return with joy.
Amen.

Proper 20

Luke 16.1–13

Gaze on an old B-movie of cowboys and Indians. The Wells Fargo stagecoach gallops over the barren Wild West of America. It has been ambushed and the driver has been shot by the bandits; he is slumped over and has dropped the reins. He can steer the coach no longer. There is a chance of safety if the horses keep together. But they dash along the rocky road and in their panic their harness snaps. They career off in different directions – one veers to the left while the other dashes to the right. Now all hope is lost. The stagecoach is heading for disaster and soon crashes to the ground. The passengers tumble out, their bones broken, heads concussed, and their luggage strewn across the hillside. The journey has ended in disaster. They will never reach their destination now.

Consider how puzzling this whole reading is. Does Jesus really expect us to admire the dishonesty of this steward? It may be that our difficulties can be explained by a mistranslation of ancient Jewish usury laws and arcane business practices, which we can no longer unravel. But however confusing it is, if we realize that this comes straight after the story of the Prodigal Son, and just before the story of Lazarus at the gate, it is clear that the part to concentrate on comes at the end – 'You cannot serve both God and Money'. You cannot place your trust in two horses that are driving in different directions. If we try, the coach that is our life will overturn and crash.

All three of these stories are stressing how our worldly concern for rank and wealth prevents our full access to God's love. For God's world runs on quite different rules to our present age. God's economy is a compassionate one, where we should always be prepared for the unexpected.

Reading this passage puts us in a very uncomfortable place, on the boundary between honesty and dishonesty, and Jesus seems to compare us with very disreputable characters indeed. At first reading we may shudder and read swiftly on. But perhaps we should pause a while and consider whether at times we don't behave like the steward, and manipulate systems for our own benefit.

Contemplate how faithful you are in the little things – in visiting a sick friend, perhaps?

Contemplate how trustworthy you are in the little things – getting a piece of work in by the deadline, perhaps?

Contemplate how honest you are in the little things – do you ever use a white lie for your own convenience, or to protect your dignity?

Contemplate how often we squander God's grace and tarnish the reputation of his disciples.

As you desire to imitate him

Dear Master, I have promised to serve you and you alone.
Help me to travel the straight path and reach my destination,
Which is your kingdom of peace and unity.
May my conduct fully mirror my ideals,
So that I will become fit to be entrusted
With your true riches.
Amen.

Proper 21

————⋅◆⋅————

Luke 16.19–31

Gaze on an icy landscape. The glacier is solid, twenty, forty, sixty feet (six, twelve or eighteen metres) deep, and so white it is somehow blue. But a chasm has opened up, wider than a person's leap. Look down into the freezing darkness. Gaze on a gorge cut by a boiling river far below. Once a bridge made of plaited bamboo crossed over, but this is worn and dangerous. See the white water surge and tumble over jagged rocks.

Put yourself on one side of the drop – you cannot stay there, you are being pursued, and somehow you must cross to safety. Can you manage this escape alone?

Consider this story as part of the long sequence we have been following that all relate in one way or another to the insidiousness of wealth and the corruption of hierarchy. Now Jesus is describing in a stark manner the consequences, and teaches us two powerful and unequivocal lessons in this passage. The first he gives in such a matter-of-fact manner: the rich man died and went to hell. Jesus passes no judgement, expounds no theory, but just allows us to draw out the inevitable conclusion, that riches and eternal life are mutually exclusive. Jesus has spent his entire ministry proving that God's compassionate economy is a reversal of the worldly order. When will we learn the consequences?

The second lesson is even more devastating. Consider how perceptive Jesus is about ordinary people. He shows the rich man caring about his family – he is not someone devoid of all feelings (but he is guilty of not having seen the beggar Lazarus as his brother too). And then consider his human response – our human response – 'Let him warn them . . .'. Jesus knows our frailty and does not suggest the rich man is much worse or more stupid that the rest of us.

But consider Jesus' insistence – he has had his chances, and has left it too late. For Jesus saw himself as the continuation and fulfilment of the prophets, who had been giving the same warning for centuries. So we learn we must listen while there is time. As with a child who always begs for one last chance, eventually the moment comes when the parent must say, 'I've told you enough times, I will not say it again.'

Contemplate how easy it is to care for your nearest and dearest, and how difficult it is to feel real compassion for the stranger. In the week ahead, contemplate what proportion of your prayer and time is spent on the stranger – is it enough?

As you desire to imitate him

Dear God and Father,
May I hear your words of judgement
And make my choice now, while there is still time.
Bless all the poor and excluded of our society,
And may I never pretend they are not there,
But treat them as I would my family.
Amen.

Proper 22

———— ·•◆•· ————

Luke 17.5–10

Gaze on this poor worker with the sweat running down his face, and blisters on his hands, plodding back from the fields. The light is dimming and he's returning to the farmhouse. How he longs to be able to bathe his tired limbs, drink cool water, and gaze at the sunset. But his master has more tasks for him to complete. The slave – for that is what he is – will not be allowed to rest until his work is done and he falls into his narrow bed for the brief hours between midnight and dawn. He'll wake next morning tired and aching and know the day ahead will be equally hard.

Gaze on the many people today, in Africa and the Far East, but also in this country too, who work in sweatshops and mines and as bonded labour. They are no freer than this slave. Hear their cries for justice.

Consider what are these 'orders' we must carry out. They are the rules by which we are expected to live: the Ten Commandments, the Beatitudes, and the Golden Rule. Jesus tells us he did not come to cancel out these 'orders' but to complete them. So we must still adhere to them and let them guide our lives. Then there would be no slaves, for righteousness and justice would reign.

But even if we ever manage to live a life unblemished by dishonour or covetousness or the worship of false gods, Jesus tells us that in itself won't get us our Lord's praise. For we would only be doing what is expected.

Considered like this, it seems to be another way of explaining that 'justification by works' is not sufficient. Though he wants us to toil for justice and work to win people for Christ, we are justified first by faith. In today's world we see all the time secular, non-believing people who live good, kind lives. But Christians are motivated by a burning love for our Master, and a willingness to give ourselves up and put ourselves last and bury our sin in Jesus' tomb.

Contemplate how often we want praise for doing our duty. How frequently relationships are marred by our insistence that our sacrifices are rewarded and our hard work recompensed. Contemplate laying down your self-centredness and becoming willing to work for others for their sake, and not for the sake of recognition.

Contemplate which fields you are called to cultivate this week, and what orders Jesus has for you.

As you desire to imitate him

Dear Master, I am your unworthy servant
And long to do my duty well.
Though I am a mere mustard seed
In the vast acres of your world,
Increase my faith and I will obey you.
Amen.

Proper 23

———◆———

Luke 17.11–19

Gaze on the people of this small border village, going about their daily business. Maybe it's market day, and rough stalls are set out selling fruit and spices. On the breeze comes the clang of bells; you hear the lepers before you see them approaching. Watch the mothers round up the toddlers, and the children run and hide, and the men stand and glare, arms akimbo, as they come into view.

Picture who are today's outcasts – veiled Muslim women stared at with disdain or the drop-out school boy who grew up unloved and seeks a family in a gang and a friend in a knife. Listen to a 90-year-old woman, the only one left of her generation in the family, who looks on and feels, 'It's not my world any more'. Gaze on all the people who don't 'fit in'; who are not 'like us'.

Consider the excellence of Luke's storytelling. We're told we're in the borderlands, but only after Jesus' healing of the ten lepers and the singling out of the solitary leper who gave thanks, is the punch line delivered: 'and he was a Samaritan' (v. 16). Consider Jesus' pity for these outsiders. He cannot abide their unloved and unlovely state. His voice alone cures them, and he tells them to go to the priests, to show them that his mission is for wholeness and rescue for all.

It is natural to care for our family and lavish our attention on them. But our family should be porous, and not a closed community. Beyond our families are the other groups we associate ourselves with. Clubs have badges, schools have uniforms, and football fans have special songs, all devices which make the group distinct and separate. Friendly rivalry is one thing, but consider how quickly it can turn to exclusion and even hatred. Racism is the greatest of these divisions, for the colour of one's skin is something we cannot take off like a badge or put in a drawer like a football scarf. We may be described by our race, but why should we be hated?

Consider why we are so defensive in the face of the outsider, and why we reserve preferential treatment for our own. Consider how Jesus is reversing this, for it is the 'foreigner' who is the one who praises God, and for Jesus this opens up the VIP entrance to the Kingdom.

Consider the response of the one who turned back, the Samaritan eager to acknowledge who has saved him, and convinced that the cure is from God. It is easy to thank someone for a simple favour, or a small gift. How much more difficult it is to thank Jesus for revoking what amounted to a death sentence – especially when the person who has cured you is from another despised group, for the Samaritans hated the Jews as much as the Jews hated them.

Contemplate living on the borderlines; think about what it is like existing between two cultures, and never quite belonging. Contemplate how Jesus came so that we would all be included in his Kingdom. When we feel 'it's not our world', and wonder why we are here, Jesus brings us to the one Kingdom where all differences will be abolished, and no citizenship test is required, except our faith. Contemplate what such a Christian community on this earth would be like.

As you desire to imitate him

Father of all, may I pity those who wander in the borderlines
    of society.
May I reach out to them with your love,
And always sing the praises of the God
Who grants to all a fresh beginning and a new life.
Amen.

Proper 24

———◆———

Luke 18.1–8

Gaze on all the people in this world who have lost heart. It won't be obvious who they are, for we are good at hiding the signs, but everyone at some time in their life will be in danger of losing heart. Then gaze on this widow, who is demanding justice. What makes her special is that she is persistent in her demand. However many times the court ushers eject her, she returns. Though she was insignificant compared to the judge, and her chances of success must have seemed slim, she believed in her cause and gained strength in adversity and kept hold of her human dignity.

Gaze on people in recent history who did not lose heart. Nelson Mandela, Martin Luther King and Mother Teresa are three great names that immediately spring to mind. They continued to struggle for peace and fairness against great powers. You may know local people who persevere against great odds. Gaze on what they achieve and give thanks.

Consider what this story tells us about the power of prayer. We have heard something similar already, in the teaching Jesus gave when he taught us the Lord's Prayer – God will hear and answer like the man who heard his persistent neighbour, the father who heard his son's plea. He is not an unjust judge.

Consider that Jesus told this story in response to an earlier question – 'When will the Kingdom come?' Jesus won't give a date or a prediction when God's justice will finally reign, but instead tells us how to behave while we wait – we are to pray.

This story also gives us a reassurance that the Kingdom will be the time when prayers for justice are finally answered.

Yet he ends on a slightly tetchy note. There is just a hint of despair in Jesus' words, 'will he find faith on the earth?' How many of us will he discover continuing in obedience and hope, prayer and persistence?

Contemplate what it means to be 'in your element'. What activity engrosses and fulfils you so much that onlookers will say 'Isn't she in her element?' As the eagle knows its element is to soar above the high mountains, and a gull abides in the harbour, and the heron in the tranquil river, so a Christian's element must be prayer.

As you desire to imitate him

Lord God, hear the cry of the dispossessed and starving.
May they not lose heart while they wait for your justice;
And teach me to persist in prayer
Until the coming of the Son of Man.
Amen.

Proper 25

————•◆•————

Luke 18.9–14

Gaze on the people in church each Sunday; think about why you kneel (if you do), and how it makes you feel. These days we no longer kneel to others, for it is a physical way of expressing humility, and acknowledging dependency.

Picture those who always sit at the back of the church 'at a distance' from the altar. Is this because they are shy, or afraid they'll be noticed? Are they ready to run out first at the end to avoid being roped in? Or do they feel unworthy to sit near the front?

Gaze at each one, and you will realize you know nothing of what is going on in their hearts. You cannot tell what sins they are confessing to, or what blessings they are thankful for. Their prayers are between themselves and God.

Consider how, in this story, the two characters we have met throughout Luke's Gospel, the Pharisee and the tax collector, are finally brought face to face in direct confrontation and comparison. This is also the second reading in a row of Jesus teaching us about prayer, and the two passages should be taken as a pair.

Consider the Pharisees of Jesus' time: by and large honourable people striving to live conscientious lives informed by their faith but cluttered with regulations. If we all lived like Pharisees we'd have reason to be proud indeed – they worshipped regularly and gave generously. What better rule of life can one have? Yet Jesus named them hypocrites.

Consider your rule of life. Or if you do not have one, perhaps now is the time to work out how you will serve God through regular prayer, study and action. But do not make the mistake the Pharisee made. Do you notice the fundamental flaw in his prayer? 'I thank you that I am not like other men' (v. 11). Instead of dwelling on his own relationship with God, he compared himself to others. In Jesus' Kingdom, we only measure ourselves against Jesus, not our neighbour, whom we judge at our peril.

Each one of us has something in our lives that means we are as guilty as the tax collector. If we rely on our own efforts, we will always fall short. Reliance on God's mercy is the only answer.

Contemplate what has become known as the Jesus Prayer – based on the words of the tax collector in v. 13 – 'Lord Jesus Christ, Son of God, have mercy on me, a sinner'.

Many people use this as their special prayer to quiet their minds and lead them nearer to Christ. Contemplate the first half which boldly states our faith, for it is a mini-creed. The second half turns to us and our relationship with God. Breathe in on 'Lord Jesus Christ, Son of God'; breathe out on 'have mercy on me, a sinner'. Breathe in God's power; breathe out your sin.

As you desire to imitate him

Lord Jesus Christ, when I am proud, humble me.
When I am self-satisfied, shake up my understanding.
When I commit sin, forgive me.
When I am penitent, have mercy on me,
For a broken and contrite heart you will not despise.
Amen.

SUNDAYS BEFORE ADVENT

The Fourth Sunday before Advent

Luke 19.1–10

Gaze on this furtive man, shinning up the tree. It is hardly dignified behaviour for such a well-off person. We are told Zacchaeus was short, so perhaps he knew that peering over the top of others' heads was not going to get him a view of the famous visitor he so desperately wanted to see. So up the tree he went.

Gaze on him sitting there very still, not moving a muscle, so that the branch does not shake or give him away. For there are other reasons why he's chosen to climb the tree – here he can see, but not be seen. His trade as tax collector makes him unpopular, to the point of being a pariah. He's not considered a fit member of society, he's labelled a cheat, and is excluded from popular company. So up here in the tree he's safe, and won't attract attention or criticism.

Zacchaeus has put himself on the margins of society and his hiding place in the tree keeps him there. Here he can be an onlooker and a bystander, not called upon to get involved. Is there room on that branch for the rest of us?

Consider how, after all the tax collectors Jesus has attracted and referred to, we finally meet one face to face and learn his name. Consider what it was that Jesus sought to restore to Zacchaeus: he had suffered a double loss, personal and social – the loss of his own integrity, and the loss of his community. That is why Jesus did not leave Zacchaeus in the safety and obscurity of the tree. Jesus gave him the opportunity to be readmitted as a full member of Jewish society.

Consider how the call of Jesus is instant and complete. We cannot stay on the margin, observing Jesus pass by. He demands all from us, or we might as well offer him nothing. Half-heartedness is not part of Jesus' plan – 'I must stay at your house *today*.'

Consider if the story had continued differently: 'And Zacchaeus hesitated, and thought about the risk he was taking, so he stayed up in the tree and didn't come down when Jesus called, but only once the crowd had passed. He tried to catch Jesus in private later on that evening, but couldn't find him. That was a pity, because he had stirred up something in him, and he felt unsettled for days. He made restitution to a few people he could remember cheating, and hoped that that was good enough. But soon he slipped back to his old ways as a tax collector. He told a few people he'd been quite impressed by that Jesus, who seemed a fair-minded kind of bloke. But by the end of the year he'd forgotten all about the excitement of the time Jesus visited Jericho. The moment had come and gone and he'd lost his only chance.'

Not much of a story, is it?

Contemplate the ways you try to hide from Jesus. Contemplate the ways you try to give him a little of yourself, and hope that is enough.

Contemplate hearing Jesus' voice calling you by name: 'Come out of hiding, take me home, I want to be your guest. For despite your weakness, I want you as my friend.' What would you have to change in your life, in response to such an invitation?

As you desire to imitate him

Dear Lord, when I hide from you, seek me out;
When my choices keep us apart
Call me back to your side,
And I will come.
Amen.

The Third Sunday before Advent

Luke 20.27–38

Gaze on Jesus – he must be tired by now, for he's been teaching in the Temple for hours, and time and again he's been questioned and even tricked. First the Pharisees challenged him over his authority, and he countered with the chilling parable of the tenants who would not acknowledge their landlord, even when he sent his son. Then he'd sidestepped the awkward question about paying taxes to Caesar, which was another attempt to catch him out and put him on the wrong side of the priests or the Romans. And now comes another sally, this time from the Sadducees, who try to ridicule the notion of resurrection. Jesus is unbowed by all these threats and tests. But he must have been so tired.

Consider if we were reading this Gospel in Lent, we might emphasize the controversy and the threat to Jesus posed by the Sadducees' questions. But reading the passage as we approach Advent, where we will consider the end of time, we are encouraged to think about God's eternal plan. Consider the kind of afterlife Jesus is describing here. Reject the vague fantasies of your childhood, and the confusion we have been left with by the advances of modern science, which have so clearly shown us what lies above the heavens. Yet wait a minute – what of Einstein's theory of relativity? What of recent descriptions of parallel universes and anti-matter? Consider the words of the Creed: if God is truly the Maker of 'all things visible and invisible', seen and unseen, we are acknowledging the mystery of other worlds, and the possibility of other states of being. There seems to be room after all for notions of eternity.

Jesus chooses not to pander to our childish urge to know exactly what life after death will be like, but rather turns to the words God spoke to Moses: 'I AM who I AM'. God is God of continuing creation, full of unending energy, and not God of destruction. In him all things are alive. And Jesus is saying that Abraham, once alive, is alive still. Once we have been lit by God's spark and our selves have been loved into being, God will always know us and cannot let us go.

Contemplate the possibility of our senses and thoughts being so overwhelmed by God's grandeur that all our attention is directed to him, and all the restlessness of our earthly life is over. The longing to recognize our loved ones is relinquished as we are caught up in worship and joy and glory.

In the resurrection Kingdom we will be in the company of our great-grandparents we never knew and our great grand-children yet to be born. In heaven we will all turn our faces towards God.

As you desire to imitate him

Eternal God, I believe in you, the Maker of all things,
Visible and invisible. So I give you thanks
For all the people I have loved,
And all those who have loved me
And are now united with you,
For in you, they are alive.
Amen.

The Second Sunday before Advent

———◆◆———

Luke 21.5–19

Gaze on the Temple again. This time look up at all the gold that burns in the sunlight, and shouts out its wealth. Look at the gigantic bunches of golden grapes adorning a central archway – each grape cluster as tall as a man. Was Herod giving glory to God when he ordered this gift, or glory to himself?

Gaze on all the gifts we bring to our churches. The apples and tins of baked beans we fetch at harvest time; the flowers gracing a wedding service, the scent of Madonna lilies wafting across the air; see the giant Christmas tree glittering in the corner. If such gifts are not brought knowing that 'of your own do we give you', then they are worthless.

Consider that here, Jesus is acting in prophet mode, and consider how desperate we humans are for prophets. We seek clairvoyants and read tarot cards and horoscopes, determined to know what is beyond tomorrow. In part this is another aspect of our great desire, or even need, to be in control. We fool ourselves that if we know what will happen and when it will occur, we might be able to prevent the worst of it, or gain some advantage. For our life is full of chance and risk and accident, and though we know that with our head, we often choose to pretend otherwise and believe we are invincible. But in reality, we must place ourselves in God's hands, in God's time, and in God's control. All we can do is live each day as if it is our last. If we were to do that, we would live it to the full; we would not bother to hoard treasure or impress others. We would want most of all to be loved. Consider how the dying words of so many people are 'I love you'. At the very end, we get our priorities right.

Contemplate verse 19: 'By standing firm you will gain life.' Contemplate standing firm *against* the temptations of this world, and against the selfish promptings of the heart, which lead us along such a false trail to power and glory.

Contemplate standing firm *for* the message of Jesus, becoming a witness for him and being given the words and wisdom to rescue the lost. Pray that today you have one opportunity to stand firm for Christ.

Then contemplate gaining life: the life Jesus means for us, lived in the power of the Spirit, lived to the full with all the vividness that it would carry if we knew it was our last day.

Contemplate this life you will gain, stripped of all human achievements, but a life in which chance has been banished, for you are sharing in the unchanging love of God.

As you desire to imitate him

Dear Lord and Teacher, may I not worry about the wheres and
    whens of life.
Instead, may I trust in your unchanging will
And speak according to your ways.
When you give me the opportunity to witness to your gospel,
May I stand firm, and so gain eternal life.
Amen.

Christic the King

---◆◆◆---

Luke 23.33–43

Gaze on the two other men, hanging on their crosses. Though we know nothing about their crimes, we may picture them as nasty, brutish men, surly, dirty and dishevelled even before this execution. Were they violent men who had spent a lifetime harming others? Perhaps they had been brought up unloved and grown a hard shell around their hearts until they didn't care about anyone, themselves included. Or maybe they had been good honest people driven to steal to feed a family, and desperate to provide for them the only way they could; provoked to rebel by the injustice of the regime. They do not protest their innocence, and one is defiant to the end. Maybe just a tiny portion of him hopes that Jesus could save them after all.

Gaze on the other one, the one who had been gazing on Jesus. What does he see there – what aura or expression could Jesus have had in the midst of this agony, to convince the criminal of his kingship?

Consider the paradoxes of this piece. We are on the last Sunday of the Church year, about to turn towards Christmas and the birth of a baby, yet here we are plunged back into Good Friday, and the death of a man. But aren't we supposed to be celebrating the Festival of Christ the King?

Consider the title 'King', and the varied associations we attach to it, some not at all helpful to seeing Jesus as our King. To us, our monarch is a more or less welcome, more or less effective figurehead who we might rally around for special celebrations – jubilees and coronations – and in times of war and crisis, but otherwise we live our lives without reference to them. Even the most ardent royalist can't pretend that our present Queen has much impact on our way of life. And for some of us Christians, some of the time, that is how we relate to Christ as King – an additional character in our world, but not someone we are prepared to accept as dominant in our lives. But it's no good to treat Jesus as that kind of king. He demands our total devotion. How far back in our history would we have to go to study a monarch who had the absolute power that we pledge to give to Jesus? None of the examples that spring to mind are very persuasive!

Contemplate just three words and ideas that spring from all we've read this year. The words are *judgement*, *love* and *reversal*. We cannot ignore the undoubted judgement of God, and the love as lived by his Son, and these must lead to the reversal of our values and way of life now we are focused on the Kingdom – on earth as it is in heaven.

As you desire to imitate him

I crown you King, with power to reign supreme in my heart.
I bow before your throne and await your judgement.
I thank you for your love and mercy,
And pledge with your help to reverse my life
Until I grow into the likeness of Christ,
My hope and my saviour.
Amen.